Secrets of Middle School

APPLESAUCE PRESS

A Girl's World Guide
The Secrets of Middle School: Everything You Need to Succeed

13-Digit ISBN: 978-1-60433-195-0
10-Digit ISBN: 1-60433-195-X

This book may be ordered by mail from the publisher. Please include $2.95 for postage and handling. Please support your local bookseller first!

Books published by Cider Mill Press Book Publishers are available at special discounts for bulk purchases in the United States by corporations, institutions, and other organizations. For more information, please contact the publisher.

Applesauce Press is an imprint of
Cider Mill Press Book Publishers
"Where good books are ready for press"
12 Port Farm Road
Kennebunkport, Maine 04046

Visit us on the Web!
www.cidermillpress.com

Design by Susan McBride. susanmcbridedesign.com
All illustrations courtesy of Cynthia L. Copeland
Printed in Canada

1 2 3 4 5 6 7 8 9 0
First Edition

The Secrets of Middle School

Everything You Need to Succeed

Cynthia L. Copeland

For Chloe

Acknowledgments

Many, many thanks to Alexandra Lewis, who provided invaluable guidance and insight as this project was being conceived and who assisted with research and interviews. Her contributions improved this book immeasurably.

A special thank you to Shelby, Ellie, Meaghan, and MaryAnn, who spent a great deal of time sharing their middle school secrets and reviewing parts of the manuscript. Thanks also to the many girls who met with us over lunch and after school and who were so honest about the challenges and rewards of being in middle school.

Dear soon-to-be middle school girl,

Starting middle school is a big step, whether you'll be going to classes in an entirely different building or a different part of your elementary school building. It may feel like a scary step, but all new adventures and experiences come with a little anxiety.

Reading this book will help you get ready for middle school, and will take away some of those nerves! You'll read all about what to do if you end up in the wrong class or if you can't get into your locker. (And you'll laugh over some embarrassing moments other middle school girls have survived!) You'll read about ways to wow your new teachers and ideas for cool things to do with your new friends! You may be a little worried about some of the physical changes you'll be going through, too, and you'll learn all about what is happening to your growing body. If you're interested, you can read tips for trying out for the school play, buying makeup, and decorating your locker! Need to talk to your parents about getting pierced ears or permission to go to PG-13 movies? Check out the chapter on home and family for advice. You'll find the answers to just about any question you might have about your middle school life in the pages of this book.

Good luck as you start an exciting new chapter of your life!

Your friend,
Cindy

What's Inside

My most embarrassing moment!! ... 8

Chapter 1

First Day Secrets: From Ruling the School to New Kid ... 11

Quiz: Are you an average middle school girl? ... 26

Chapter 2

Secrets About Friends and the Social Scene ... 28

Secret ways to fold and pass notes ... 48

Chapter 3

Boy Secrets ... 50

The secret meanings of dreams ... 70

Chapter 4

Secrets from the Classroom ... 74

Great websites for girls ... 95

Chapter 5

Secrets About Parents and Life at Home ... 96

Middle school girls in action ... 113

Chapter 6

Body Secrets ... 115

What does your zodiac sign say about you? ... 142

Chapter 7

Secrets About Life After the Bell Rings ... 144

Middle school bucket list ... 166

Chapter 8

Secrets from Girls Who Are Older and Wiser ... 168

My Most Embarrassing Moment!!

Lots of girls have embarrassing moments in middle school! Until someone invents a time machine so that you can go back and avoid the goof-up, the best way to handle the occasional *OOPS!* moment is to laugh along with everyone else! Just act like it was as funny to you as it was to your friends and classmates, and then put it behind you as quickly as you can. Chances are, everyone will follow your lead and move on.

In the middle of a math test (when everyone was totally quiet), I got a horrible case of the hiccups. The more I tried to stop them, the worse they got! They were super loud and weird sounding because I was trying so hard to cover them up. I was hoping that everyone would just forget about it as the day went by, but two periods later, in the hall, I overheard this guy from my class telling a bunch of his friends about it!
-B.L.

At the end of the year, there's always an awards ceremony in the auditorium. I wasn't expecting to get anything, so I was talking quietly to my friends. All of a sudden, I heard my named called! I stood up and went running up on stage... except that they hadn't called my name, but a girl whose name sounds a lot like mine. I didn't realize it until we were both standing on stage. The walk back to my seat was the longest walk of my life!
-K.B.

Our school band got new risers that were a lot narrower than the old ones. During our first concert in front of the entire school, I was sitting on a stool playing the piccolo and I shifted my position. The leg of the stool went off the edge of the riser and I fell backwards! It was one of those falls like in the cartoons, where the person's arms go flailing backwards like a windmill. I didn't get hurt, but I was so embarrassed!
-A.H.

My mom and I were shopping together at a department store. She's really small and loves fashion, so we actually share clothes sometimes. I was looking through a pile of jeans and found some to try on. My mom was looking through a rack of clothes and had her back to me. I said, "Hey, Mom!" but she ignored me so I poked her in the shoulder and said, "Mom!" again. When she turned around, it wasn't my mom at all but a girl who wasn't that much older than me! She looked at me like I was crazy! I just sort of slunk away, but I wanted to say, "You should see my Mom! She's really pretty and young looking...that was a compliment!"
-C.K.

We were all working on our English essays and so the class was totally quiet. All of a sudden I had to sneeze – not a problem, but I made a very loud fart at the same time! My friends will not let me forget that!
-T.C.

I had a huge crush on this guy so I stuffed a note into his locker asking him if he liked me. Only problem was that it wasn't his locker! It was this totally geeky guy who is a grade younger than me! By the time I realized it, he had already read the note and showed all of his friends.
-P.L.

Our PE class was held outside because it was nice weather. We were jogging around the soccer field and I had just caught up with this really cute boy when I felt something on my head. I reached up to touch my hair and felt this gooey blob – BIRD POOP! EW! I got it all over my hand! The boy was so grossed out that he hasn't talked to me since!
-N.L.

Once in math class I knocked over my water bottle and the water spilled onto my pants. Of course, the spill made it look like I wet my pants. The teacher let me go to the office and call home, but my mom wasn't there. I called my grandma, and she brought pants in for me... but the pants were these weird purple stretch pants she had at her house that she thought would fit me! I couldn't wait for that day to end!
-E.D.

I was rushing to get to the bus in the morning so I grabbed a shirt and a pair of pants out of the dryer and threw them on. When I was walking down the hall at school I heard people snickering. I didn't think about it until I met up with my BFF at my locker and she told me that – thanks to static cling – I had a pair of underpants stuck to the back of my pants! It would have been bad enough if they were just plain underpants, but they were my little sister's Dora the Explorer underpants.
-S.R.

I was showing this cute guy how I can squeeze through the space in a chair between the seat and the back part but I got stuck! I could always do it in fifth grade so either the middle school chairs are smaller or I got bigger! The janitor had to come and unscrew part of the chair. That's what you get for showing off, I guess.
-S.G.

For the first middle school dance of the year, my mom made me wear a really fancy dress and she curled my hair. She convinced me that all the girls would be wearing the same type of thing. Of course, everyone was in jeans and I looked like something out of a Disney movie (and not in a good way!). I hid in the bathroom for the entire night and my best friend brought me snacks and told me what was happening at the dance!
-M.D.

I went to the movies with a group of my friends. About halfway through the movie, I went to the snack bar to get popcorn. I thought I knew exactly where we were sitting and would have no trouble finding my seat, but when I walked back into the theater it was pitch black. I felt around until I

touched a seat and counted to the row I thought we were sitting in. I eased myself into the seat on the end. Suddenly I realized that I was sitting on someone's lap! I apologized and got right up, then whispered to my friends until they answered me from a couple of rows away. When the movie was over, I looked back to see whose lap I had sat on and it was this cute high school guy who was with his girlfriend. Of course it couldn't have been some nice, understanding motherly type.
-A.L.

I was late and running for the bus last year when I tripped and fell flat on my face! And of course my stop is the last one so the bus was full and everyone was staring out the windows at me!
-T.G.

When I was a little kid, I told everyone at school that Johnny Depp was my uncle. I have no idea why I said that, except that everyone did want to be my friend for a while. Of course, since then I admitted that I made it up, but kids still tease me about saying it, which is so embarrassing.
-T.F.

My older brother put a really weird ring tone on my phone without telling me. I took my phone to school but forgot to put it on vibrate. In homeroom, the teacher was reading announcements and all of a sudden my phone went off! It was bad enough that I got in trouble for having my phone on, but all the kids in my class thought I picked that dorky ring tone!
—C.C.

Chapter 1

First Day Secrets: From Ruling the School to New Kid

In your last year in elementary school, you ruled! After all those years in the same place, you knew which bathroom stall had the best lock, you had at least three good strategies for snagging an indoor recess when it was freezing cold outside, and you didn't really need a hall pass because all of the teachers knew you weren't a troublemaker. It was so familiar, so comfortable… almost too comfortable, right? There were probably times that last year when you looked around and felt too old to be in elementary school. You felt ready to move on, ready for new challenges and experiences.

Now, here you are in middle school! Even though you feel excited about that, you probably feel nervous, too. With change comes anxiety. There's no getting around that. But adjusting to your new surroundings won't take very long, and there are a few things you can do that will make that adjustment period easier. Sometimes, just thinking ahead and planning how you would handle a certain situation if it came up can make you feel more relaxed. And if you know what to expect in the first days and weeks, you'll be able to prepare.

Starting middle school offers a lot of opportunities you might not have considered. First of all, it is a chance

"I couldn't believe how old some of the kids looked in middle school! I mean, I saw a kid who was almost as tall as my dad and had an actual moustache! Seriously! But there were also a bunch of kids who looked too young to be there. I was surprised at the wide range."
—Keisha

"No matter how confident other kids look, everyone is a little freaked out on the first day! My friends and I talked about this at the end of sixth grade. None of us wanted to admit how nervous we were because we thought we were the only ones!"
—Faith

to make a fresh start. Do you want to break away from a previous image you didn't like and redefine yourself? Maybe everyone from your elementary school had labeled you as a crybaby or a complainer. You can think about the reputation you'd rather have and start school by focusing on making a positive change. What about your friendships? You can expand your circle of friends to include girls who share some new interests you may be developing, whether in cheerleading, drama, or computers. Lots of interesting choices will help you discover what you enjoy and where your talents lie, whether it's

Some Things Never Change

A lot of things will be different in middle school, but a lot of things will be the same. Unfortunately, some of the things that you wish would change, don't!

Things That Will be Different

- You'll have a different teacher and classroom for each subject. (Think of the upside here: That teacher you don't like so much? You only have her for 45 minutes a day—not six hours!)

- The teachers will expect more of you, but they'll also treat you like young adults rather than like little kids.

- You won't have recess, although you'll have a lunch period and maybe a study hall to chill with friends (and lots of cool after-school clubs and sports for socializing).

- Your backpack will be heavier. (Ugh.)

> "I walk a mile to school and my textbooks are SO heavy to carry back and forth everyday. I asked my teachers if they had extra books so that I could keep one at home and one at school. Two of them found extra books for me!"
> —Samantha

- You'll stash your stuff in a locker instead of a cubby in a classroom.

- You won't know everyone in your classes (at first).

Things That Will be the Same

- Boys will think that jokes about boogers and farts are hysterically funny. Ha ha.

- You'll be able to smell your way to the cafeteria. (And the hot dogs are still more like rubber than actual food.)

- The cute boy whose last name starts with the same letter as yours will end up nearby in places like homeroom and gym class.

- Everyone wants the bathroom pass at the same time, like when the guidance counselor visits health class to talk about "I Care" language.

- Come Sunday night, you'll wish you had started your homework on Saturday.

delivering the morning's news or weather on the school's television station or taking photos for the yearbook.

When you eventually go back to elementary school to visit your old teachers, you won't believe how little the kids look—even the fourth and fifth graders! And you'll think, "Wasn't I bored spending all of my time in the same classroom with the same people?" You'll feel like you've grown up a lot in a short period of time.

"A really nice girl in my neighborhood who is two years older than me gave me a tour of the middle school about a week before school started. It was so helpful to walk around and figure out where everything was (like the bathrooms!) without a million other kids in the halls."
—Kiki

"I love being one of the new kids in middle school because you have the 'well, I'm only a sixth grader' excuse if you don't know something, like where a classroom is. I just joined the soccer team because I figure no one will expect me to lead the team to victory or anything like that, but if I ever do, they'll be so happily surprised!"
—Chloe

Locker Secrets

Here's your locker:

14

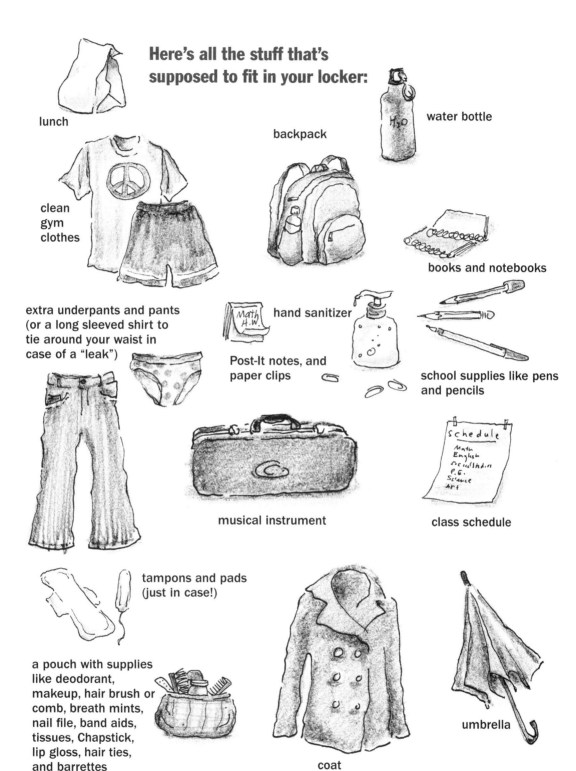

Here's all the stuff that's supposed to fit in your locker:

lunch

water bottle

backpack

clean gym clothes

books and notebooks

extra underpants and pants (or a long sleeved shirt to tie around your waist in case of a "leak")

hand sanitizer

Math H.W.

Post-It notes, and paper clips

school supplies like pens and pencils

musical instrument

Schedule
Math
English
Social Studies
P.E.
Science
Art

class schedule

tampons and pads (just in case!)

a pouch with supplies like deodorant, makeup, hair brush or comb, breath mints, nail file, band aids, tissues, Chapstick, lip gloss, hair ties, and barrettes

coat

umbrella

What you DON'T Want to Keep in Your Locker...

old lunches

anything expensive or breakable

smelly gym clothes

"My friends and I 'mail' notes to each other by sticking them through the little open slots in the lockers. It's totally fun, but we have to be careful that we get the right locker! Otherwise it could be a disaster!"
—Sofia

What if ...

...your locker isn't anywhere near your classes or it's too high or too low?

Talk to your homeroom teacher or guidance counselor about switching. The first week is a busy one for everyone, so if you feel your request may have been forgotten, continue to visit the guidance counselor in the weeks to come: Be persistent but polite. In the meantime, see if you can find someone who would be willing to switch with you. You'll always have better luck if you approach an adult with a solution as well as a problem.

... you can't remember your combination or can't work the lock?

Come up with a rhythm to remember your combination, like you would a phone number. If you're concerned before you start the new school year, you can buy a combination lock over the summer and practice using it. (You'll probably have to use the school-issued lock for your locker, but at least you'll get used to how one works!)

...you can't tell which one is your locker in the endless row of lockers?

Believe it or not, you will be able to zero in on it no prob in a few weeks. But initially, until you get used to exactly where it is, put a tiny sticker or magnet on it so that you can pick it out right away.

…your locker partner covers your locker with pictures of Hannah Montana which totally embarrasses you because you haven't liked her since third grade?

Be nice. She just doesn't understand that Hannah Montana is a little young. Suggest that because it's a shared locker, you should come up with a theme you both like. Maybe you'll never agree on a band or a celebrity, but you can probably come up with a color that you both like. Tell her that if she wants to stay after school sometime, you'll help her take the HM pics off of the locker and make them into a cool collage that she can use as a binder cover instead.

…you think your locker partner is helping herself to your stuff or being unkind?

First of all, take home anything that is valuable to you and try to time your locker visits so that you don't have face-to-face contact. Then make an appointment to talk with your guidance counselor. Your mom or dad can send an email to the counselor before you meet, explaining your concerns. That way, he or she knows you've spoken with your folks and have their support. Your counselor should find another locker for you as soon as possible.

Secret Place to Write your Locker Combination

Begin to tear the back page of a notebook and stop when it's about a third of the way out. Fold the top part of the page down. Write the combination in such a way that the numbers are half on the folded-down part of the page and half on the other part. The marks won't make any sense to anyone else when the page is unfolded but you'll be able to double-check the combo when you need to!

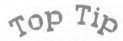

Ask permission before trading lockers. Some schools do random locker searches and you don't want to get in trouble for something that isn't yours!

Decorating Secrets

A lot of girls find that decorating their lockers is one of the most fun parts of middle school! You can express your personality and celebrate your interests in this part of the school that is all yours. (Before you begin, check the school handbook to make sure your decorations won't land you in detention!)

Many girls find that choosing a theme or a favorite color helps guide their decorating choices. What have other girls put in their lockers to make them special?

"A magnetic peace sign, a magnetic pencil case, and a mini disco ball!"

"Notes from my friends and photos of my friends and my family."

"A picture of Obama and a battery operated light so I can see what's in there."

"Pics of David Beckham and the Beatles."

"Penguin wrapping paper on the sides and a magnetic basket to hold stuff."

"Drawings I did of my dog and characters from Tim Burton movies."

"An old coffee can that I decorated for holding pens."

"I hate being late to math class, so I visit my locker the period before and do the combination on the lock just up to the final number so that it will open with one small, final turn when I swing by on my way to math."
—Nina

"A digital clock magnet and a cork board for tacking up notes."

"An air freshener and a pair of fuzzy dice!"

Idea!

Tape a large piece of paper to the inside of your locker so that your friends can sign it and write short notes. When it's full, take it home and save it in your memory box and then put up another one!

"Stars (that are really Christmas ornaments) that hang from the ceiling."

"Little magnetic stuffed animals and a magnetic pen and pencil holder."

"Fuzzy fabric for the bottom of the locker and the shelf, and magnetic clips with googly eyes on them."

"A mini calendar, magnetic hooks for keys and stuff, and a white board."

"A magnetic holder for my makeup and one for my cell phone."

"A mirror with a magnetic strip on the back and some really cool magnets."

Fun FAcT

"A poem I wrote, a white board that opens up to be a mirror with lights, and a picture from the newspaper of my crush playing soccer."

According to a recent poll on GirlsLife.com, more than half of the girls who responded said that clothes take the top slot on their back-to-school shopping lists! While sixty-three percent of girls are spending their money on clothes, less than a quarter say that school supplies top the list and about 14 percent say makeup and accessories are their first back-to-school purchases.

Cool Things to Make for Your Locker

- Anything can be a magnet! Just attach a strip of adhesive magnetic tape or glue a small magnet on the back of a mounted photo, favorite quote, cool piece of sea glass, or fun button.

- Decorate a small mirror with felt and foam cutouts. You can also add sequins and other craft store items.

- With adhesive magnetic tape, attach a piece of beaded fringe to the edge of the shelf.

- Cut the back pocket off an old pair of jeans (including the part of the jeans it's attached to). Glue magnets to the back of the pocket and decorate it with paints and patches and use it to hold pens and pencils.

- Attach a piece of adhesive magnetic strip to the back of a small notebook or an old CD that you've decorated with a photo collage. (Check out the scrapbooking section of your local craft store for ideas.)

"I love having a locker—it's like having my own personal little closet space right in the middle of the school."

—Alex

3 Tips for Keeping Your Locker Organized

1 Have a specific place for everything and make it a habit to put things where they belong every day so that your locker never gets completely out of control. This means that you won't waste precious time between classes looking for the right book or notebook in the pile at the bottom of the locker.

2 Clean your locker out every few weeks using this system: Take everything out and sort the items into three piles: "throw this away," "take this home," and "put this back neatly" (if you need it for school).

3 Use things like shelves and shoeboxes to keep supplies organized, as well as magnetic organizers specifically made for lockers.

Idea!

See if the student council or your homeroom wants to organize a locker-decorating contest!

Surviving the Bus Ride to School

Before you get to middle school, you may have to ride on the middle school bus! With 50 or so pre-teens packed into a tight space supervised by one adult who is also trying to drive, the bus ride may be a little crazy. But there are definitely ways to survive the ride, and maybe even enjoy it!

Bus DOs and DON'Ts

DO play games on your cell phone or listen to music on your iPod! Listen to your fave songs or watch that episode of Gossip Girl that you downloaded last night.

DO a last-minute review for a test by bringing flashcards and having friends quiz you! (Definitely don't try to juggle loose-leaf notes or a big, bulky binder on your lap, but a few small flashcards could be a great use of your bus time.)

DO get to know your bus buddies. It sounds obvious, but be friendly to the people in the seats around you. If they ride your bus, chances are they live close by, so it might be nice to have some friends within walking distance!

DO play Would You Rather… That's the best bus game around.

Make Sure You DON'T Make These Mistakes!

DON'T save homework for the bus ride! Even if your bus ride is outrageously long, you will just be frustrated if you try to get homework done. You have no space to work, you can't concentrate when you're surrounded by noisy kids, and it's just not a great idea to save work for the morning that it's due.

DON'T sit in the back. The farther you are from the driver, the more likely it is that you'll be surrounded by troublemakers.

DON'T play Truth or Dare. You don't want to have to follow through on a crazy dare that will get you kicked off the bus.

You may have an OOPS moment or two during your first few weeks in middle school. Don't panic—handle it with humor and confidence and you'll come out looking better than if it hadn't happened at all!

What if...

...you can't get into your locker?

If you're on you way to class, forget about getting into your locker and get to class on time. Explain to the teacher that you weren't able to get into your locker and ask her if you can share a book with someone else for the day. (Bonus: You might make a new friend!) Most middle school teachers are very understanding for the first few weeks. If you do have time to address the stubborn locker, find the person who assigned you the locker (maybe your homeroom teacher) and ask him to troubleshoot the problem with you.

...you walk into the cafeteria and have no idea where to sit (and who to sit with)?

Plan ahead. Hook up with someone who is in your same class right before lunch. Walk in with her and sit together the first day. It will take a few days to figure out who you know in that lunch period and what table your friends will grab. Within the first week, you'll find a group to sit with. (Score some good karma points by including your "first day friend" if she hasn't connected with a group yet.)

...you sit down in the wrong classroom?

A very common mistake. Come up with something clever to say, like, "Well, I just wanted to say 'Hi' to all of you before I went to my REAL class!" Then just get up with a smile, head to your guidance counselor's office, ask him where you're supposed to be, grab a hall pass, and get directions to your class.

Top Tip

The best way to avoid having kids make fun of you is to beat them to it: Make fun of yourself first.

22

> "I was SO thrilled that my best friend from elementary school was in all of my classes in sixth grade! While all of my other friends had to branch out and make new friends, she and I stuck together. Unfortunately, when I started seventh grade, she was only in one of my classes and I really hadn't made any other friends. I think it's best to jump in from the first day and make friends when everyone is new, too."
> —Amelia

...you can't find your bus at the end of the day and you miss it?

Another case where planning ahead will help. Form an alliance with someone who takes the same bus you do: "Let's meet at the main office as soon as school is over and walk to the bus line together!" Put your heads together and try to find the right bus. If you miss it, there's a 50/50 chance you won't have to call your mom for a ride because your friend can call hers!

...you get on the wrong bus?

Don't just get off at some random stop! Tell the bus driver that you are on the wrong bus. (If you have a cell phone, let your parents know what's happening.) Maybe the driver will be going back to the school once he's dropped everyone off (or maybe he will take you back there at the end of his route). Ask him to wait and make sure you can get back into the school building. Once you're there, you can call your parents or another adult you know to take you home or you can take the late bus home.

...you blank on your schedule and can't remember where you're supposed to be?

That won't happen if you buy binders with see-through covers. Slip in a copy of your schedule (and a map of the school). No one will even know you're confused because you can just glance casually at the front of your binder (instead of fumbling through your backpack) and figure where you're supposed to be and how to get there.

...you don't have a single friend in any of your classes?

Sorry to sound harsh, but this is a "buck up" moment. It's your chance to make new friends. If you had a best friend in all of your classes, you wouldn't have any reason to make new friends, and eventually everyone would know lots of different people except you! (A sincere compliment like "I love your haircut!" is all it takes to get a conversation going with someone you don't know.)

"Don't shop for back to school clothes until after you start school and can see what other girls are wearing! I bought these really cool flared stretch pants with pink roses on the bottom that I thought would be so hip and cool in middle school. When I got to school on my first day, no one was wearing anything like that so I refused to wear them ever again even though they were kind of expensive. My mom was so mad at me!"
—Josie

...your special first day outfit shows up on someone else?

You can still create a unique look! Take off a layer, roll up your sleeves, pull back your hair to show off an attention-getting necklace or change into that spare T-shirt you have in your locker. Remember, though: You and your "twin" are probably the only ones who will really notice. Everyone else is too busy worrying about their own clothes to pay a lot of attention to others!

...the teacher doesn't get your name right, or uses your full name instead of the nickname you prefer?

Politely correct her on the first day. During the first roll call, rather than saying "Here" you can say, "Actually, I prefer Katie." Or, if you feel uncomfortable doing that, go up to her right after class and tell her what name you'd prefer or how to pronounce your name. Get it out of the way on the first day so that she doesn't get used to calling you by the wrong name.

"The very first day they announced sign-ups after school for sports and activities. I almost didn't go because I just wanted to get home and crash. But I made a friend go with me and we signed up for cross-country, the school TV station, and the robotics club. I'm so glad I forced myself to jump right in because then I really felt like a part of the school."
—Carmen

Ask your friends to take this just-for-fun First Day
Would You Rather Quiz!

On the First Day of School, Would You Rather...

...go to school wearing a prom dress OR a dirty, torn sweat suit?

...trip and fall on your face in front of your crush OR accidentally trip your crush (except that he doesn't think it was an accident)?

...accidentally oversleep and miss the first day of school OR get someone else's schedule so that you go to all the wrong classes for the entire day?

...go through the whole day with something in your nose OR pass gas (not silently) in homeroom?

...have a horrible new haircut OR have your dad pick you up right after school on a riding lawn mower?

...have your teacher catch you passing a private note and read it aloud to the class OR find out your math teacher is your archenemy's mother?

....laugh so hard at lunchtime that you start choking and hack up some of your food OR spill ketchup down the front of your shirt (and have no way to clean or cover up the stain)

...call your teacher "mom" in front of the class OR get called to the main office because your mom brought you mittens and a hat because she was afraid you'd be cold walking home after school

Fun FAcT

A survey of more than 2,000 girls by an organization called Girls, Inc. found that even though many girls worried about being teased (41 percent), getting good grades (82 percent), or how they look (32 percent), more than 60 percent of the middle school girls said that they were happy at school, had lots of friends, got good grades, and got along well with their parents.

QUIZ
Are You a Typical Middle School Girl?

1 Have you had more than one relationship with a boy?

2 What's more important in a BF: a sweet personality or looks?

3 What's your favorite snack?

4 Are you part of a clique?

5 If you're in a clique, is it the "cool" clique?

6 What's your favorite kind of book to read?

7 Books or movies?

8 Where does most of your spending money come from?

9 Do you wear makeup?

10   Lip gloss or blush?

11   Do you like your fingernails long, with polish,
or short, with no polish?

12   Bell bottoms or straight legs?

13   Daddy's girl or Mommy's girl?

14   What is your favorite rainy day activity?

15   McDonald's or Burger King?

Did every one of your answers match the answers most commonly given by other middle school girls? If so, you are a typical middle school girl! If you're not a **statistically average middle school girl***, you are an interesting, independent, out of the ordinary middle school girl, which is just as great!

The Average Middle School Girl says:

1. No
2. A sweet personality
3. Ice cream
4. Yes
5. No
6. Romance
7. Books
8. Allowance
9. Yes
10. Lip gloss
11. Long, with polish
12. Bell bottoms
13. Daddy's girl
14. Watching TV or a movie at home
15. McDonald's

*According to online surveys

Chapter 2

Secrets About Friends and the Social Scene

Let's just get it out there: The trickiest part of middle school can be the social scene. Girls you could always count on for fun in elementary school suddenly ignore you. Your soccer teammates from last year don't seem to care about sports anymore; now they're all about makeup and boys. Your new group of friends decides that in order to be with them, you have to ditch your old group. Ugh.

Not to worry: You can definitely handle it! By knowing a few secrets, your friendships can be the **best** part of middle school! After all, looking ahead to a Friday night Drama Club party or a Saturday sleepover with your best friends can make a week of math quizzes and social studies homework fly by!

Secret number one: Forget about trying to please the "cool" crowd. The problem with that group in most middle

> "From the very first day, always smile and be nice to everyone. Don't spread rumors or gossip about other girls. Stay as far away from the drama as you can. The best reputation you can have is to be the 'nice girl.' If you can float between crowds and have lots of different friends, that's the best way to go through middle school!"
> —Alyssa

> "It was hard at first. Every single ittle thing that I did seemed to affect my rank in the social hierarchy. One girl I had always been nice to in elementary school because everyone else thought she was weird suddenly became popular and she decided she was too cool for me. But within the first couple of weeks, I met two girls who were good, true friends and we stuck together all through middle school."
> —Elena

schools is that the kids can be fickle and mean. One day you're in, the next day you're out. That's just too stressful. You need friends you can count on for support and for fun.

Secret number two (which is tied to number one): Try hard not to worry about status or rank in middle school social life. It's a crazy system that no one has figured out and no one probably ever will. A kid who you remember sucking his thumb in fourth grade is suddenly everyone's go-to guy. What's that about? And the girl whose mother asked you to come over two years ago because she had no friends is now the "it" girl. Why? Because over the summer she got blonde highlights and then she made the soccer team? Maybe… No one knows. Middle school "status" is a mystery.

Explore different friendships without worrying about what other kids think. It doesn't matter if your cheerleading friends don't understand why you also like to hang with a bunch of girls from Art Club. Just do your best to avoid girls who are unkind and focus on treating everyone as nicely as you can. You want to find a few true friends who will stick up for you when you're not around and make you laugh and feel good when you are around.

> "I'm kind of embarrassed that when I first got to middle school, I followed this girl Kim everywhere. I was a total cling-on. I know it kind of freaked her out, but she was the first friend I made and I didn't know anyone else. I wish I hadn't acted so desperate and needy, because now I have lots of friends and I'd like to re-connect with Kim but she definitely keeps her distance. I should have had a little more confidence in myself."
> — Violet

> "I used to have this friend who liked to make 'helpful' comments that were really put-downs in disguise. When I would tell her that she hurt my feelings, she always got all huffy and said she was just trying to help me. I was like, 'Is it me?' Then I thought about it and I realized that she really was being nasty! I moved on to my new friend Kara, whose helpful comments are actually meant to help me, not hurt me!"
> — Trenese

"Friends" Who Really Aren't:

- Friends who copy off your homework or test

- Friends who borrow money all the time and don't pay it back

- Friends who are jealous (instead of happy) when something good happens to you

- Friends who tease you in a way that makes you feel bad

- Friends who make you feel bad if you don't have as much spending money as they do

- Friends who spill your secrets

- Friends who always go after your crush

- Friends who use you to get into your "crowd"

Secret number three: Look at middle school as a great opportunity to bond with girls who have the same interests you do. In elementary school, you were friends with kids who lived on your street or who were in your class. Now you can find friends who are a lot like you. What do you love? Math? Lacrosse? Music? Drama? Find clubs or activities that allow you to explore things you really enjoy. Be cheerful and friendly to everyone and you'll start to make connections. Ideally, you will keep some friends from elementary school and make new friends in middle school.

If you've had the same friends for years, your social skills might be a little rusty! But connecting with wonderful, new friends is easy because they want the same thing you do! Just about everyone is looking to find new girls to hang out with. Chances are, if you ask a question ("I love your shirt! Where did you get it?") or just start a conversation ("That solar car project we're doing next week is going to be pretty cool, don't you think?"), you'll find someone who is eager to respond. Just steer clear of anything negative. Don't make fun of someone else or complain about the teacher. Keep it upbeat, and be the kind of friend you would like to have! If you think you've found someone you'd like to get to know better, offer to save her a seat in lunch or ask if she wants to be partners with you for the next lab in science.

"At the first meeting of the Drama Club, I noticed this girl, Dawn, who I immediately decided was super snobby. She sat down in the corner of the room and she didn't talk at all. I ignored her for about a month and so did everyone else. Then the advisor put the two of us together in an improv exercise. It didn't take long before I realized that I had totally misjudged Dawn. She is such a sweet person, just very, very shy. After that, I made a promise to myself that I would not pass quick judgments like that again. I consider Dawn one of my really good friends now."
— LaKeita

"You have to accept that there are some kids who just won't like you, for no reason at all. In some cases, they're just jealous. Don't let it bother you. Focus on all of the kids who do like you and don't let the other ones even get on your radar screen."
—Bailey

Don't be discouraged if you don't make a connection right away. Keep trying. Everyone is nervous at first and that anxiety manifests itself in different ways. Some girls are overly talkative but others might clam up and come across as aloof or strange. Don't write anyone off, but for the time being, just move on to someone who is more receptive. If nothing else, you'll start to build a reputation as someone who is open and friendly. And look on the bright side: If it takes you a while to find someone in class to talk to, the teacher will just think you're a very focused student who refuses to be distracted!

"I brought extra school supplies with me the first couple of weeks. When someone forgot a pencil or needed a paper clip, I always offered up one of mine. One of my best friends is a girl I gave extra notebook paper to on the second day of school!"
—Paige

Now and then, you'll have to problem-solve some issues that arise with friends, some silly, some serious. Your best bet is to take the time you need to think things through so that you feel confident about the way you handled a given situation.

What if...

...you need to "break up" with a friend?

Awkward! First of all, think hard about why you're ending the friendship. Make sure your reasons are good and sound. If they are, the most important thing to consider is the old Golden Rule: How would you want someone else to treat you in the same situation? You need to be kind and thoughtful. It will be hard enough when she realizes that you don't want to be her friend anymore. You don't want it to be even more painful because of the way you handle it. You can explain that your time is really limited with your academic and extra-curricular commitments and that you find yourself doing things with girls who are involved in the same things you are. You can tell her that you have great memories of the things you've done together and you hope she does, too. Remember: You want to end things on the best note possible because you may decide a

> "Now that I'm a couple of years out of middle school, it's interesting to see that some of my friendships that fell apart in middle school were rekindled in high school. Girls can be pretty weird and even mean in middle school, mostly because they're insecure. But most of that disappears in high school as everyone gains confidence and direction. Try not to get entangled in a lot of negative stuff and never write someone off entirely."
> —Julia

> "I like having some friends at a different school because when I need to vent about someone, I can do it to my friends who don't go to my school now. I don't have to worry that they will repeat what I said or think it's weird if the next day I make up with the girl I've been arguing with."
> —Mindy

year from now that you'd really like to be friends with her again. (If a friend "breaks up" with you, move on quickly and graciously. Your feelings may be hurt, but remember: There are lots of other girls who'd love to be your friend.)

...you end up at a different middle school than a lot of your friends from elementary school?

There's always texting, IMing, Facebook, and phone calls to stay in touch on a daily basis. On weekends, make plans to have sleepovers so you can catch up. Just think of all the different stories you'll have to tell each other about what's happening in your lives! In time, you may want to start including some of your new friends so that everyone can get to know each other. Another great way to guarantee that you'll keep in

touch with your old gang is to promise to get together for each other's birthdays. Somehow, people find ways to hang on to the friendships that mean the most to them as they bring new friends into their lives. This happens throughout life as people change schools, move, switch jobs… You may lose touch with some people, but great friends always find a way to get together and be part of each other's lives.

Top Tip

One of the best ways to make new friends quickly is to join a sports team.

...your BFF turns into a copycat?

Of course you already know that imitation is the sincerest form of flattery. When someone else goes out of her way to dress like you, talk like you, and get her hair cut like you, it must mean you're pretty great! A lot of girls are insecure in middle school and are trying on a lot of different personalities and looks to see what feels right. If you can help your friend to feel more confident, she might be less inclined to copy you. When she wears or does something that is original, compliment her! Point out her great color choice or cool dance moves. If that doesn't work and things just feel too weird, try to make a joke out of it (that also will let her know you're a little uncomfortable): "OK, so I'm planning on wearing my black striped shirt tomorrow, so you'd better go for something else or people are going to think our mothers are dressing us alike!"

....your closest friends don't like each other?

This happens to adults, too, and it's always hard to figure out. Sometimes it's as simple as jealousy. Each of your friends wants to have you to herself but they all have to share you—and they keep hearing all of these great things about the other one! You are thinking you want everyone to be part of one big, happy group, but each of your friends wants to be the only one! And sometimes the problem is as simple (and as complicated!) as a personality conflict. If you can't bring your friends together, then you'll have to do things separately. And your best bet is to try not to talk about one with the other—it will make them less likely to become friends, not more likely.

...you and your BFF like the same boy?

Let her have him, or decide he's off limits for you both. It's not worth losing a friend over a boy. Even if you start dating him, it could be over in a week or two, but she could be your good friend ten years from now. Other girls will see that as a mark of loyalty and will think of you as a true friend. (If you go for it, and get the boy, you may find your BFF and her other friends try to make you feel pretty guilty about it.)

Fun FAcT

Almost 3,000 girls responded to an online survey asking what they would do if they and a friend both had a crush on the same boy...

- 42 percent said they would let the friend have the guy

- 40 percent felt like they should both find different guys to avoid ruining the friendship

- 18 percent would go after the boy and tell the friend to back off

Tattling
versus Telling

You are tattling if you tell a teacher something just so that another kid gets into trouble. Your goal isn't to help anyone out, but to make someone else look bad. You are telling if you report something to a teacher or parent because you feel it will help someone out. Your goal is to keep something bad from happening.

…one of your friends starts making some really poor choices?

You don't want to "tell" on a friend. That's always the dilemma. If she realizes that she's getting in over her head, urge her to talk to a trusted adult. Suggest people she might want to talk to like a favorite teacher, your mom, the school nurse… If she doesn't see that there's a problem, then you have to decide how serious it is. What's the worst thing that could happen to her? If she could end up getting badly hurt or getting into serious trouble, then you will need to confide in someone. Try asking a relative, teacher, or guidance counselor about the situation without using your friend's name. You can tweak the facts a little so that you get advice without betraying your friend's confidence. If it's so serious that you need an adult to intervene, find someone you trust to handle the situation so that your friend gets the help she needs but your name stays out of it.

"It can be hard to give a friend advice without sounding preachy. But sometimes my friends do dumb things! My strategy is to casually mention a made-up person doing the same (dumb!) thing to get my point across. I talk about what happened when my 'other friend' cheated on a test and got caught, or when my 'other friend' got in tons of trouble for shoplifting, or whatever the issue is. It works best when I'm talking to a third person and the friend I'm worried about just happensto be within earshot."
—Kara

Tired of Being the SHY ONE?

Tackle your shyness in baby steps. Don't try to become the talkative, outgoing girl overnight. Start with small goals, like smiling to the person sitting next to you in math or complimenting the girl who has a locker next to yours. Before each encounter, rehearse it in your mind. Think about what you'll say and imagine things working out well.

If you feel yourself starting to blush, slow things down and take time to calm yourself. Don't avoid the situation that is making you blush; just take a deep breath and confront it in a more relaxed way. Take control of your imagination and picture a positive outcome.

...your friendships with guys start to have a crush vibe?

You don't have to date every guy you like. Friendships with guys last longer and are less complicated than dating relationships. Sometimes middle school friendships turn into high school romances because you've had a chance to build a great foundation for a relationship. For a lot of kids, the best part of a relationship is before there actually *is* one: when things are fun and flirty but not full of concerns about how far to go and whether he'll call you. Try to keep things low key with a guy friend by including other kids in your plans so it doesn't feel like dating.

"My best friend is a guy. When he got a girlfriend, we stopped hanging out. I was really bummed out but when they broke up after a couple of weeks, we started doing stuff together again. It's exactly the same with my girlfriends— as soon as they start dating someone, they have a lot less time for their friends. I see how quickly couples break up, so I'm always going to put my friends first."
—Lola

...your BFF is acting like someone you don't know?

Middle school is a time when everyone is trying to understand herself better. Kids want to stand out with unique identities but also fit in with everyone else. It's a confusing few years. You might watch one of your friends quit the swim team to hang with kids who are into Japanese anime and another one ditch her preppy clothes in favor of Goth get-ups. If their experiments are harmless, try to be understanding and supportive. Continue to expand your circle of friends, looking for girls who are interested in the same things you are.

...girls you thought were your friends are suddenly acting mean?

If you can ignore them and just hang out with other girls for a while, that's probably your best option. That lets the mean girls know that they don't have the power to make your life unhappy. If unkindness turns to bullying, you need to let a teacher or counselor know about it.

...you really don't like the boy your BFF is hanging with because you've heard he's a cheater or a loser?

You don't want to ruin the friendship, which means you have to be really careful. First of all, make sure you know the facts about this boy and are not just getting sucked into gossip and rumors. If you have evidence that the guy really is a jerk, then look for an opportunity to steer the conversation in that direction. If she mentions something he did that was unkind, prod her to talk about it. Ask lots of questions and try to help her come to the same conclusion you did.

Three Cool Things to do With Your New Friends

Come up with some fun rituals and traditions for your new group of friends that will help solidify you as a group. Here are some ideas:

1 Have a pants party!

Visit a thrift store together so that every girl can buy a pair of cheap jeans. (If you don't want to decorate jeans, you can buy inexpensive canvas bags at a craft or fabric store and decorate those.) Back at your house, scrounge some craft supplies like puff paint, ribbons, buttons, iron-on patches, glitter, and permanent markers. Turn up the tunes and go crazy decorating the jeans. Be sure to write special messages on each other's jeans. Every time you wear them, you'll all think of each other!

"We like to decorate jeans together because the kids on sports teams sign each other's jeans at the last event of the season as a bonding thing. So having signed jeans is a cool thing. We also like to decorate book bags by writing our favorite quotes on them and writing special messages to each other."
—Amy

2 Find a place that is "yours."

Scope out a place within walking distance of your school that you can call your own. After school, meet there and hang out at "your place" with your friends. It might be a place that has the best chicken wings and root beer in town, or a place that plays jazz music, has student artwork on the wall and has different kinds of tea.

"There's a place called Brewbakers right downtown and we walk over after school and get hot chocolate and a muffin or cookie. We sit at this big booth in the back and talk about everything that happened at school. It's fun to do because when we were in elementary school, we had to either leave school on a bus or with a parent. Now we can just go by ourselves!"
—Savannah

All that matters is that it's a safe, fun place to spend an hour after school with your buds!

3 Pass around a friendship journal.

Disguise your journal as a subject notebook. Determine a rotation among your group of friends and then begin writing entries and passing it along to the next one in your group. It's like a group diary! You can catch up on everything that's happening with your BFFs throughout the day. Leave the margins free so that the others can make comments, give feedback, or add stickers!

> "The worst was when one of our friends would start dating a guy she really liked and ignore all of us the entire time they were going out. She'd alienate everyone. Then, when they broke up, she'd come crawling back and pretend like nothing had happened. We'd get SO mad at her"
> —Crystal

... "everyone" gets invited to a party except you?

As tempting as it is to walk up to the girl having the party and ask her why you weren't invited, don't do it. You want to be above that. If she excluded you to be mean, you don't want to let her know that it bothered you. Don't play that game with her. Make a plan with other people for the evening so that if someone asks if you're going, just say, "I have plans with my friends from gymnastics tonight." Afterward, when people are talking about what happened at the party, listen with a smile, and then change the subject at an appropriate time.

> "My advice on friends? Groups of three just don't work."
> —Dede

Peer Pressure

In elementary school, peer pressure was often a good thing! That kid can read a chapter book? Hey, I want to do that! He made a diorama with an appliance box? Cool! I'll try it next time!
In middle school, though, when kids have a bit more independence and are starting to feel more adult, peer pressure takes an uncomfortable turn. Some kids want to grow up more quickly than others, and their idea of what "grown-up" means can be very different from yours.

> "Yeah, there's pressure from certain kids to drink. Whatever. I have enough personality to have fun without doing anything stupid or illegal and I just feel sorry for the kids who need that stuff to have fun."
> —Meg

You want to fit in. You want to have friends and be part of a special group. *Who doesn't?* But sometimes the cost of being friends with a certain person or group is just too high. You want to feel comfortable and relaxed when you're with your friends, not anxious that you will be pressured into doing or saying things you don't want to.

When you are feeling conflicted about whether to go along with the group, force yourself to think about the consequences of what you're doing. Sometimes, the worst thing that could happen is not that bad. If your friends urge you to wear black eyeliner, you might try it and realize that you like the natural look better. Or if they want you to listen to a band you don't think you'll like, all you lose is the time it takes you to listen to a few songs on your iPod. No biggie. Sometimes, though, a consequence could have lasting implications, like if you get caught stealing from a store or smoking a cigarette. You would develop a reputation you don't want, your parents wouldn't trust you for a long time afterward, and some of the kids you might really enjoy being with wouldn't want to be associated with a troublemaker.

> "I'd never been to the mall before and I was finally going on a big shopping trip with one of my friends. Lisa told me that if I didn't get some clothes from Abercrombie she wouldn't be friends with me any more. So I spent tons and tons of money on things I didn't even like. A few weeks later she decided that she didn't want to be friends with me anyway."
> —Ellie

> "In my school, there's a ton of pressure to buy all Abercrombie and Hollister stuff. But my friends and I like to go to thrift stores and put together our own funky outfits that don't look like anyone else's! I think it's dumb to spend a ton of money just for a certain brand name. To me, it just shows that you don't have confidence in your own taste and style!"
> —Milena

As you get older, you'll be confronted more and more often with these kinds of dilemmas. It's just part of growing up. As you make your own decisions, you are starting to write your own life story and determine your own destiny. Ask yourself if you feel good about the decisions you're making and about

Fun FAcT

The results of a peer pressure survey by smartgirl.org revealed that peer pressure can be positive as well as negative: 69 percent of girls often feel pressured to expand their horizons by experimenting with different kinds of food, music, or movies, and 68 percent often feel pressured to get better grades. On the negative side, 67 percent often feel pressured to look a particular way, and 44 percent often feel pressured to lie, steal, or cheat. A quarter of those responding often felt pressured to use drugs, alcohol, or cigarettes.

"A lot of my old friends began hanging with the 'in' crowd. I could have done that, too, but I decided that I was more relaxed doing stuff with this other group of girls who weren't considered quite as cool, but who were thrilled to do things with me. For three years, we did so many fun things together and we were always there for each other. I never regretted my decision to seek out my own group who liked me exactly the way I was and didn't try to make me do things I didn't want to do."
—Julia

the direction your life is taking. Are you still in control of your own life and your own choices? As long as you are, you're on the right track. If you begin to feel like you are doing things that are uncomfortable or just not "you," then you need to make some changes. Compromising your integrity just to keep a few friends is not what you want to do. People of all ages tend to respect those who are true to themselves, not those who blindly follow. If you act with confidence, and not apologies, then you will gain the respect of your peers. Find a group where you can be the leader, not a follower. Then lead in a positive way.

Idea!

Some schools have special days when everyone walking into the lunchroom gets handed a random table number and must sit at the assigned table. It's a great way to make new friends! If your school doesn't do this, suggest it!

HOT OR NOT?

We asked real middle school girls to give us the 411 on lunchtime. Things may be different at your school, so don't take the list *too* seriously.

What's hot: Veggies or fruit and dip (healthy, easy to share, delicious!)
What's not: Skipping lunch

What's hot: Hot lunch, if the menu is good, like pizza or chicken fingers
What's not: Messy dinner leftovers or an overly-complicated lunch that requires you to assemble it at the table

What's hot: Homemade cookies to dole out at the end of the meal
What's not: Making a huge pile of garbage that you have to clean up at the end of the meal

What's hot: Mints for after lunch
What's not: Food that smells bad at the table (or in your locker) or that gives you bad breath afterward, like hard-boiled eggs or tuna fish

Lunchtime

Lunchtime! At first, it can be a little nerve-wracking trying to figure out where to sit, what to eat, and who to eat with! You might have had assigned tables in elementary school, and now in middle school you can choose where you sit. This might cause a little anxiety at first, but you will find some friends to sit with, or you'll make some new friends. It won't be long before lunch is not stressful at all, but a really fun part of the day. It's a chance to catch up with your buddies and relax a bit. Now that you've moved on from Lunchables in a Strawberry Shortcake lunchbox, you're ready for more sophisticated food *and* conversation!

Top Tip

Bring a lunch on the first day because the hot lunch line can be very long as kids figure out the drill. You don't want to end up with only 5 minutes to eat your mystery meat!

"Walk in with a friend and claim a table with confidence. Don't stand there looking around waiting to see who might want you to sit with them."
—Jamica

"Don't be the girl who doesn't eat lunch. No one thinks it's cool and you won't be able to focus all afternoon. Plus, after school you'll pig out because you'll be starving!"
—Jackie

"I had kind of a bad first day because I had forgotten to take out my retainer before going to lunch. When I took it out at the table, it had those saliva strings on it and everyone was grossed out. Plus, for some reason, my retainer says Adam on it and for a week afterward my friends called me 'Adam.'"
—Molly

"If someone asks you to share, you have to. Otherwise you look stingy. If someone offers to share with you, you *have* to take it. Otherwise you seem too picky. Even if it's a *booger*... Well, maybe that's an exaggeration..."
—Danielle

Mean Girls

Are you going to be the girl who listens in on a sneaky three-way phone conversation (remember that scene from "Mean Girls"?) or the one who invites the girl to your sleepover who hasn't been able to make a lot of new friends? It's your choice. It comes down to the same Golden Rule you probably learned in kindergarten: Treat other people the way you'd like to be treated. It may seem hard to believe sometimes, but you will be liked and respected by more girls (and by the right type of girls) if you treat people with kindness. In fact, make a special effort to smile at, talk to, and include girls who seem to be the victims of mean girls. You have no idea how much a kind word can mean to someone who is being teased.

You don't want to be a mean girl… *but* you don't want to be a victim either. How can you avoid being harassed by the mean girls? Take the advice your parents give you when your brother starts teasing you: Ignore it, and don't let on that it bothers you. It's that easy.

Top Tip

Come up with a comeback that won't get you in trouble! Sometimes using humor or a bit of sarcasm can help!

Don't allow yourself to be a victim. Look confident and strong. Remember what former First Lady Eleanor Roosevelt said: "No one can make you feel inferior without your consent." Simply ignore any snickering and whispering—turn to a friend, say something to her, and then laugh together. Walk away from anything mean and join up with another, more welcoming group.

> "It's really hard not to get caught up in the drama. I remember once Chloe took Emily away from me and she wouldn't include me because she said I was 'different.' Emily became, like, Chloe's accessory. Then one day, Chloe decided that she didn't like Emily anymore so she just tossed her aside. Emily went from following Chloe everywhere to not even being allowed to talk to Chloe."
> —Abby

Victims tend to be the ones who hang on the fringes of the mean cliques, hoping to get noticed. So from the beginning, do what you can to keep your distance. That way, you're off their radar screens. Most groups have a certain spot in the school where they hang out. Walk right past those kids and float among the groups of nice kids.

If you ever feel that teasing gets out of control, you'll need an adult to

"The popular group in my grade tried to make my life miserable. They made fun of the fact that I didn't want to make out with boys. But I made friends with a really sweet girl named Brie who was looked down on because her family didn't have a lot of money. We had a blast doing things together and I knew she would never turn on me and suddenly be mean. I could relax with her and tell her anything without worrying that she'd blab it to someone else. The two of us were friends all through middle school."

—Analee

intervene on your behalf. Keep track of what happened when so you can report the facts. Your parents, a teacher you trust, your guidance counselor, or your school nurse are good choices. With an adult's help, you can problem-solve some coping strategies or perhaps change homerooms, lockers, or gym classes to help you keep your distance from troublemakers. Adults who work in middle schools are aware of the social problems that can arise and have helped to resolve lots of issues similar to yours. If you don't connect with the first person you talk to, get in touch with someone else who will be more helpful.

"My friend from elementary school, Rachel, was jealous of my new friend Faith so she called me and Faith 'lesbian lovers.' We ignored it and just tried to be nice to her because it's hard to be mean to someone who's always nice to you. After a while, she just stopped."

—Leah

What Is Cyberbullying?

Cyberbullying is using the Internet to taunt or hurt someone, like leaving mean comments on MySpace or Facebook. Never take part in this kind of behavior and tell your parents if anyone ever does it to you.

"I noticed this girl from my bus stop was being bullied. I didn't want to get into trouble with the girls who were being mean, but I wanted to help her somehow. I left a note on my teacher's desk about exactly what happened but I didn't sign my name."

—Cara

BFF QUIZ

How well do you know your BFF? Fill this out as if you were her, then ask her if you got the answers right!

SCORING:

13 to 16 correct answers: You know your BFF as well as she knows herself...maybe better!

9 to 12 correct answers: You know enough about your BFF to order for her at a restaurant or to pick out a movie that she would love!

5 to 8 correct answers: You may want to spend some more time with your BFF!

1 to 4 correct answers: Are you sure she's your BFF?

I can't live without my _____

The funniest thing that happened to me this year was

_____

_____

If I could be an animal for a day I'd be a _____

The first thing I notice about a boy is _____

In 20 years, I'll be _____

If I could choose a superpower, it would be

_____

My greatest fear is _____

The person I dread sitting next to in class is

_____

My favorite treat is _____

The place I most want to go is _____

My most played song in iTunes is _____

The subject I really hate to have homework in is

_____

My favorite color nail polish is _____

If I had $20, I would _____

The craziest thing in my backpack is _____

If I became famous, my stage name would be

_____

Do You Really Need a BFF?

Maybe you do, maybe you don't! It can be great to have that one best friend to share secrets with, talk to on the phone for hours, sit with at lunch every single day... But there will be times when you're between best buddies, and that's ok, too. You can't force a BFF relationship. Sometimes it's really fun to have a few good friends instead because you won't panic if your best friend is home sick or moves to a different school. If you are lucky enough to have a true BFF, be sure to nurture other friendships, too. And if you don't have one, relax and enjoy all of your friendships for what they have to offer.

Fun FAcT

When asked about the most stressful part of middle school (given the choice of workload, activities, friends, or teachers), 26 percent of the 3,600 girls who responded said that dealing with friend drama is the most stressful.

When It's Your Friend's Birthday...

- Make posters to hang up in school with a pic of your friend and her "posse" that says: "**If you see** _____ **today, wish her a happy b-day!**"

- Decorate her locker with streamers and notes on her b-day!

- If the b-day kid is a boy (who is a good sport), you can embarrass him a little bit by cutting out a pic of his face and putting it on a bikini model photo and hanging it up near his locker!

New Friends

So ... you probably have stuff written all over your hands, notebooks, and book covers so that you won't forget your new friend from social studies or cross-country. Before you lose track of that important info, jot it down here. (Bonus: When you flip back through the pages of this book at the end of middle school, you'll remember how you met all of your buds and what your first impressions were!)

Name: _____

Cell #: _____

Home #: _____

Address: _____

_____

_____

I met her in _____

_____

The first thing I noticed about her was

_____

_____

I think we'll be good friends because

_____

_____

Name: _____

Cell #: _____

Home #: _____

Address: _____

_____

_____

I met her in _____

_____

The first thing I noticed about her was

_____

_____

I think we'll be good friends because

_____

_____

Name: _____

Cell #: _____

Home #: _____

Address: _____

_____

_____

I met her in _____

_____

The first thing I noticed about her was

_____

_____

I think we'll be good friends because

_____

_____

Name: _____

Cell #: _____

Home #: _____

Address: _____

_____

_____

I met her in _____

_____

The first thing I noticed about her was

_____

_____

I think we'll be good friends because

_____

_____

Name: _____

Cell #: _____

Home #: _____

Address: _____

_____

_____

I met her in _____

_____

The first thing I noticed about her was

_____

_____

I think we'll be good friends because

_____

_____

Name: _____

Cell #: _____

Home #: _____

Address: _____

_____

_____

I met her in _____

_____

The first thing I noticed about her was

_____

_____

I think we'll be good friends because

_____

_____

Name: _____

Cell #: _____

Home #: _____

Address: _____

_____

_____

I met her in _____

_____

The first thing I noticed about her was

_____

_____

I think we'll be good friends because

_____

_____

Name: _____

Cell #: _____

Home #: _____

Address: _____

_____

_____

I met her in _____

_____

The first thing I noticed about her was

_____

_____

I think we'll be good friends because

_____

_____

Secret Ways to Fold
and Pass Notes...

Homeroom is a great place to make friends because the
rules aren't quite as strict as they are in other classes.
Here's how to fold and pass notes in homeroom so that
no one will notice.

Folding

Here is THE cool way to fold a note when you're in middle school:

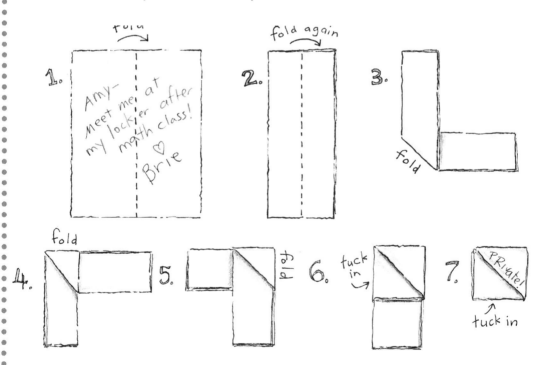

Passing

• Put your graphing calculator in letter mode and type out a note. Show your friend the screen as if you were revealing a math equation or lending her your calculator.

• Put a note inside the cover of a book and pass the book over.

• Write a message in your HAB (homework assignment book) so it's like you're showing someone your homework.

• If your friend sits behind you, add a note to a pile of papers from the teacher that you are passing back.

• Go to the pencil sharpener or bookshelf and drop a note near your friend's desk along the way.

• Crumple up a note and toss it toward the trashcan so that your friend can pick it up and "throw it away."

• Tuck a note under the cap of a water bottle or wrap it around inside the label (which is usually just glued on one corner) and pass the bottle to your friend.

• Slide a note under the top case of your calculator.

• Ask your friend if she's cold, then tuck a note into your sweatshirt and pass it over.

• Unscrew a mechanical pencil (where you'd fill it with lead) and put the note inside.

• Stick a folded note inside the clip of a pen.

Chapter 3

Boy
Secrets

Middle school boys aren't as much of a mystery as you might think. It's true that boys don't usually talk about their feelings as much as girls do, so it can be hard to figure out what's going on in their heads. But you can tell by their actions and the choices they make what's important to them. In general, boys mature later than girls, so they can seem a bit more childish. While a middle school girl may be thinking about finding "the one," a middle school boy is probably thinking about being first in line to buy the newest video game or wondering whether he'll be cut from the basketball team.

Some middle school boys (like some girls) just aren't interested in dating or relationships yet. Girls can seem a little scary to 11 and 12 year old boys. If *you're* afraid to put yourself out there, imagine how a boy feels. If a girl has her heart broken, she may run to the bathroom to cry while her friends rush to comfort her. It's different for boys in our culture. They're (unfairly) expected to be tougher, and not to show as much emotion. Can you picture a boy crying in the bathroom with his friends after getting dumped by his GF? And yet a boy who has been rejected by a girl is just as sad as a heart-broken girl. So some boys are understandably uncomfortable with the whole dating idea and choose to put it off in favor of doing things with their friends.

> "It really hurt my feelings when I asked this guy out and he said yes, and then a couple of days later he changed his mind. But that was over a year ago and he hasn't had a girlfriend since then. So I guess it wasn't really about me, it was more that he wasn't ready to date in general."
> —Charlotte

Six Secrets About Boys

1 Most boys are very uncomfortable with "girl drama" and really don't like it when girls say mean things about other girls.

2 Most boys think girls spend too much time trying to get boyfriends and should pursue their own interests more.

3 Most boys don't like it when girls wear tons of makeup and uber sexy clothes.

4 Most boys would rather have a confident girl who feels great about herself than an insecure one (no matter how pretty) who needs a lot of compliments.

5 Most boys worry a lot (privately) about their own hair, clothes, and skin.

6 Most boys find girls confusing: They think it's hard to tell when girls are just being friendly and when they are hoping to get asked out.

> "I had a huge crush on this new boy at school. If I saw him in the hall or at lunch it made my day. Then one night, he called me! It freaked me out so much that I totally ignored him the next day in school. It was way more fun as a crush than as an actual relationship! I'm sure he was completely confused."
> —Allison

Many middle school boys, however, are interested in having a girlfriend, or at least in going out on group dates. They'll be more open to getting to know different girls. If you'd like to get the attention of a certain boy, there are a few secrets you should know. Boys, like girls, are attracted to positive, friendly people, so put your happiest face forward. Confidence is also a big turn-on for guys. If you make it clear that you think you're a pretty terrific person, other people will think so, too! That doesn't mean being stuck up, it just means having the confidence to be friendly to everyone, to be proud of your talents, and to be true to the person you are.

> "I think that boys don't like it when girls seem really needy and desperate for boyfriends. They like girls who have interesting lives and have lots of things going on because they are freaked out by the idea of being the center of some girl's universe."
> —Kelsey

Never change things you like about yourself to appeal to a particular boy. If he likes quiet girls and you're outgoing, find another guy! The problem with trying to be someone you're not is that you just can't keep it up! Sooner or later, the real (wonderful!) you will come out, so it's important to connect with someone who is naturally a good fit so that you can both relax and enjoy being together.

Another secret: Mean girls don't appeal to most boys. They know that it's just a matter of time before those kinds of girls are mean to them, too. This is where the reputation you developed as a nice, kind person will really help. If a boy realizes you like him and he asks other people what you're like, you want the report to be a good one.

Fun FAcT

Thousands of girls were asked if they felt they were **boy crazy** and only 15 percent said YES! For 13 percent, boys weren't on their minds at all, while 72 percent said *... kind of.*

Find out as much as you can (on the DL) about the boy you're crushing on. Does he like a certain band, or author, or sport? You'll want to find out if you have common interests so that you can start a conversation about something you both like. Ask lots of questions. Boys—like girls—love to talk about themselves! If it turns out the chemistry isn't there after all, maybe you will have made a new friend.

> "'Going out' with a boy in middle school basically means that you slow dance with him at the dances, he sits with you at lunch, you pass notes (that don't really say much), you sit together on the bus, and you talk about when you'll break up."
> —Cara

> "I sent one of my friends to ask this boy if he liked me, but she did it when he was standing with a bunch of people and he said no. So now I'm not sure if he really doesn't like me or if he was just embarrassed in front of his friends."
> —Malia

> "I wrote a short note letting my crush know I was interested in him. I didn't make it too mushy in case anyone else saw it. I wanted to give him time to think about things and not put him on the spot. Maybe tomorrow I'll just casually go up to him and ask if he got the note."
> —Sarah

TOP TIP
Avoid extremes:
Don't ignore him;
don't stalk him!

What Does it Mean to "Go Out" with a Boy When You're in Middle School?

"Going out" means different things to different kids, but in general it means that you might sit together at lunch, talk at your locker in the morning, talk on the phone after school, or dance together at the school dances. It might last a day, a week, or a month, but for a middle school couple to last more than a few months is rare. For preteens, "going out" is a way to start learning a bit about the opposite sex and taking small steps toward more serious relationships in high school.

If you find out there is a spark, and you want to ask him out, the best idea is to casually invite him to join you and your friends if you are going to a sporting event, fast food restaurant, or party. You'll have some moral support from your buds and be more relaxed than if you two were alone, so he'll get to know the real you. (And your parents might be happier with this arrangement, too!)

Now… there are going to be times when the boy you like isn't interested in having a relationship with you. (And

Mean Boys

Yep, there are mean middle school boys just like there are mean girls. Mean boys are angry and insecure just like mean girls are. Putting another person down somehow makes them feel better about themselves. Feel sorry for people like that, and avoid them whenever you can.

If a boy teases you, roll your eyes and walk away, or laugh with your friends and shake your head. Give the impression that he just isn't worth even responding to. Act bored, not upset. By doing that, you may shut him down faster than if you ignored him completely.

If the teasing ever gets very mean-spirited or heavy-handed, don't hesitate to involve an adult. That's bullying, and schools have strict policies against it. You will have lots of support from teachers and other adults in school if you report that type of behavior. Write down some notes about exactly what was said or done (and when) so that you can be specific when you seek help.

there will be times when you aren't interested in a boy who has a crush on you.) People are drawn to others for reasons they might not even understand themselves. If the guy you have a crush on doesn't feel the same way, it's not about who you are, it's about whether he feels it's a good match. Zac Efron likes Vanessa Hudgens right now, but that doesn't mean that Ashley Tisdale isn't amazing! It just means she's not right for Zac! If your crush tells you he's not interested, move on as quickly as possible, with dignity. Accept his feelings and take another look around: There are a lot of great guys out there! And after all, you will date many, many people before you find "the one," and every encounter gets you closer to figuring out the type of guy you really like.

Fun FAcT

Of 16,000 parents responding to an online survey, 39 percent do not allow their middle schoolers to date; 20 percent allow it only in groups. About one-fourth of parents do allow dating. (Fifteen percent said that their kids weren't interested so it wasn't an issue.)

> "If someone is being nasty, I try and come up with something funny to say. If I can get people to laugh, usually the person who is trying to be mean gets frustrated."
> — Vivienne

> "One time this girl was mean to me in math class and I went up to her locker afterward and asked, 'Are you having a bad day?' She actually looked like she was going to cry and said, 'Yes.' I told her that I hoped things got better. She never bugged me again."
> —Lauren

> "You have to stick up for your friends. I was friends with a really nice girl whose eyes were kind of crossed. These boys walked by our lunch table making their own eyes crossed and laughing. My other friends and I went right over to their table and told them that that wasn't ok and to leave her alone. Maybe it's because there were four of us and we're tough, but they didn't bug her again."
> —Sasha

What Is Bullying?

Bullying is when someone repeatedly uses words or actions in an effort to be unkind or hurtful. It's not about specific things that are said or done. It's about the intent of the bully and the fact that he or she makes someone else feel frightened, upset, or uncomfortable.

What if....

...your friends don't like your BF?

Why don't they like him? Is it because they are jealous that you are spending a lot of time with him that you used to spend with them? If so, you'll want to make sure that you spend time doing things with them to show them that they are still important to you. Or is it because they truly feel that he is not good for you? Maybe they don't know him all that well. Ask them to be honest with you and then take time to think about what they say. They may be concerned for your safety or happiness. That would be something to take seriously. (If they just think he is a dork, that is not a reason to end a relationship that makes you happy!) Try to assess their concerns objectively before deciding whether to stick it out or move on.

> "It's amazing what you can see when you're not the girlfriend."
> —Susannah

> "This girl Kari was always making fun of my boyfriend and the kind of clothes he wore. After a while, it got to me and I broke up with him. He is dating a really great girl now, and I'm so upset that I let Kari influence me. She was really just jealous that I had a nice BF!"
> —Cassie

...you are way more interested in boys than your friends are?

It's okay to be into boys, as long as it doesn't become more important than schoolwork, activities, and friends. You need to strive for balance in your life. The problem with being too boy crazy is that you can't control much of what happens with relationships and so you are putting yourself in a position where you will have lots of ups and downs based on whether the boy you like smiled at you, or didn't, or asked you out, or broke up with you. You can't control other people's feelings and actions. If you have a lot of different interests, you will be able to make sure the things that are within your control are awesome and make you feel great about yourself.

...you just don't feel ready to date boys yet?

You have many years of dating ahead of you. Don't worry if right now you'd rather draw, hang with your little brother, or ride your bike instead. You'll be an adult for a long time; enjoy your last few years of being a kid! In the meantime, develop some friendships with nice guys. You'll begin to feel more comfortable hanging around with them, setting the stage for dating in the future. Join some activities that interest you where you are likely to run into girls who feel the way you do. Never force yourself to grow up faster than you want to.

"When my friend Jen starting dating Dan I was so upset because she knew I liked him! I was ready to stop being friends with her forever! I'm so glad I kept my feelings to myself because they only dated for like two weeks and she's still one of my best friends. And it turned out he was kind of a jerk."
—Stephie

...you're tempted to talk trash about one of your friends because you're competing for the same guy?

This is bound to backfire. Your crush will think you are a bad friend and mean person. And your friend could find out what you said. You're better off going to your friend and talking to her honestly about the situation. You might both agree that the friendship is more important than the boy.

...you have a huge crush on a guy who doesn't know you exist?

How well do you know this guy if he doesn't even know you exist? What often happens is that we develop a fantasy of what someone is like based on a little bit of information. We tend to fill in the blanks the way we want to, not in a realistic way. So enjoy the crush for what it is—more like a crush on a celebrity than feelings for a real person who has flaws.

"When I want to get to know a certain boy, I just make sure to casually cross paths with him whenever possible in the hallway, near his classes, and after school. Once he's started to notice that we've been bumping into each other for a week or two, then I'll start saying 'hi' to him every so often. After a while, I'll throw out a question or make a funny comment about some activity or class. Pretty soon we're friends, and he thinks it just happened naturally!"

—Monique

"My friends and I have crushes on celebrities more than we do on boys in school. (Middle school boys can be kind of gross.) We don't get too carried away, but we have their pics in our lockers and on our binders. There's no chance of rejection, but we tell ourselves there's always the remote chance that we could meet our celebrity crushes and they will fall for us!"

— Annie

...you're not sure whether to tell your crush how you feel?

It's scary to have a crush because when the relationship is just in your head, the fantasy is great! But once the word gets out, one of two things will happen: either he'll like you back (YAY! YAY! YAY!) or he won't (leaving you with a temporarily broken heart). You do have another choice, though: Just keep the crush to yourself and enjoy it like a fun little secret! Maybe knowing that you'll see him in math class gives you something to look forward to all day! Or thinking that you might catch a glimpse in the hall makes going from class to class an exciting adventure! It might be best to keep it to yourself unless you get signals from him that he feels the same way.

...a guy has a huge crush on you and you're just not that into him?

How would you want someone to treat you if the situation were reversed? It took a lot of guts for this boy to tell you how he feels. Someday, you *will* be on the other end and you'll want to be treated kindly. It is possible to be caring, while also being firm and clear so that he won't continue to pursue you. You can say (or write in a note if it's easier), "I'm glad you told me how you feel and I'm really flattered. I think you're cool, but I'd rather just be friends. I'm sure you'll find a great girl who will want to be your girlfriend."

TOP Tip

Don't let a crush on a teacher or other adult get too serious. You should think of it like you would a celebrity crush, just something fun to think about. You *never* want to cross the line of appropriate behavior with an adult.

HOT OR NOT?

What's hot:
Double dating or group dating
What's not:
Odd numbers on a group date

What's hot:
Taco Bell or a fast food restaurant
What's not:
A fancy restaurant

What's hot:
Hanging out with a group of friends
What's not:
Hanging out alone in your boyfriend's bedroom all the time (you don't want a bad reputation)

What's hot:
If your guy remembers your one-week anniversary
What's not:
If you make a big scene because your guy forgot your one-week anniversary

Girls on Boys

Girls have lots to say about middle school boys and dating. Do these girls say the same kinds of things that your friends say?

Mary Ann: "Having guy friends is more rewarding than flirting with everyone and trying to have lots of boyfriends. My guy friends like me because I'm real around them and just act like myself. I'm not trying to act 'flirty' around them."

Janie: "Middle school boys have sweaty hands. It's gross."

Meg: "Stay away from any boys who are possessive or clingy."

Katie: "There's nothing wrong with going out with boys in middle school as long as you don't take it too seriously. I mean, it's not like you're going to marry one of these guys!"

What Does "Butterface" Mean?

Some middle school girls use this unkind term to refer to a boy who is great in every other area but is not good-looking. (Just fyi: Surveys show that most pre-teen and teen girls feel that looks are somewhat important, but are certainly not the most important thing.)

Camilla: "If there's a guy you want to date, definitely be friends first. Otherwise it's just awkward! But if you break up, make sure you can still be friends, otherwise that totally stinks!"

Nina: "Dating in middle school isn't worth all the drama! Hanging around with good girlfriends is way more relaxing and fun most of the time. No worries!"

Palmer: "Everyone wants to have a boyfriend just to say they 'have' one. How many people actually care about the person they are supposed to be in a 'relationship' with?"

Pia: "People should have boyfriends just to make friends and hang out with cool people. It's lame when girls have boyfriends just so they can brag about dating in middle school."

Kiki: "I want to wait until high school when the boys don't act like such little kids."

Deanne: "You can make some really good guy friends if you handle the dating thing the right way. If I didn't date Johnny, we probably wouldn't be friends now."

Caryn: "I didn't date at all in middle school and I turned out just fine! No one thought less of me, and I had more time to build great friendships with my girlfriends that are still really important

to me. I am dating in high school because now I'm ready."

Mariah: "Girls should start out having guy friends. Then you get to know how guys think and why they do and don't like certain girls. When you're ready to date, you'll feel more comfortable with guys."

Amber: "Sometimes a boy will date a certain girl just to improve his own status, but you wouldn't want to date a guy like that."

Tina: "I think boys like girls who are friendly and girls they can relax with, not girls they have to impress all the time."

Ways to Tell if a Guy Likes You

- He finds random reasons to talk to you.
- He gets so nervous that he doesn't talk to you at all.
- He flirts with your friends so you'll think that he's desirable.
- He flirts with you.
- He calls you on the phone… but it's about homework.
- He never calls you on the phone.
- He teases you.
- He's ignores you completely because he's embarrassed that he likes you.

(Can you tell by this list that there really are no sure-fire ways to tell?)

What Type of Guy Is Perfect for YOU?

Find out what kind of guy would be your dream date!

Start ➔ I imagine I'll be able to count on my dream guy to …

give me butterflies

make me laugh

My favorite books to read are…

romances

true stories

cheer me up when I'm sad

at a dance

The way I imagine I'll meet my dream guy is…

in math class

having a nice dinner, just the two of us

My idea of a perfect date with my dream guy would be…

through mutual friends

going to a funny movie

I know my dream guy and I will share…

the same fun hobbies

the same sense of humor

60

My dream guy will make my heart beat faster when he…

touches my hand when I'm not expecting it.

The Sweet Guy

The Sweet Guy is considerate and supportive. You can count on him for a kind word and for good advice. He's always there to listen and help. (And if you share a secret, he'll keep it.)

raising a family

sends me amazing letters about how he feels

The Sophisticated Guy

The Sophisticated Guy has a lot of confidence and seems older than a lot of other middle school boys. He is a leader, and he sets the trends; he doesn't follow them.

In 20 years, I will be…

working at an amazing job I love

travelling all over the world

The Fun Guy

The Fun Guy likes to joke around and have a good time. He teases you, but in a way that lets you know that he likes you. He tends to be at the center of any group, the boy everyone is drawn to.

61

Secrets of Middle School Dances

ADMIT ONE TO A VERY FUN DANCE!

Middle school dances are a great way to hang out with kids from school without any of the school stuff like classes and tests! Dances can be even better than parties at a friend's house because you can get to hang with kids who aren't in your close circle of friends. So if there's someone you've been wanting to know better, dances are a great opportunity!

> "Go with the attitude that you're going to have fun. If you plan on standing in the corner looking awkward, you'll feel like an outcast. This is one of the times when joining the crowd is a good thing."
> —Tori

Some dances are held at the school to celebrate a holiday like Valentine's Day, while others are community events, held somewhere other than school, like at a Rec Center or church building. These other dances might be open to kids from other area schools. Some dances are for all middle school grades, while others are limited to a particular grade. Often, flyers are sent to the schools announcing the details. Get as much info as you can so that your parents will be comfortable dropping you off at events that aren't at the school. Sometimes, a police officer will help chaperone. That might make your parents feel better about you going.

> "My parents didn't want me going to Rec Center dances at first. Then we talked it over and worked out some rules that I promised to follow if they'd let me go. The big one was not to leave the dance for any reason. I also had to agree to let them pick me up an hour before the dance actually ended and be waiting by the door. I also promised to reply to their texts right away. It's kind of a pain, but at least I get to go."
> —Benita

In some cases, there will be tickets on sale ahead of time. During lunch or after school, kids or parents will have a table set up to sell tickets. Sometimes, the older kids are allowed to buy tickets first, in case there aren't enough for all students to attend. (Sometimes it helps to keep $5 or $10 in a special place in your backpack for times when you suddenly realize that you'll miss out if you wait until you bring money the next day.) In other cases, you might pay at the door.

> "Our church sponsors dances every month. Because I'm in the youth group, I can get in by bringing a six-pack of soda. I have to help clean up afterward, but a few of my friends are in the youth group, too, so we talk about what happened at the dance while we sweep and pick up."
> —Ebony

If you don't like to dance, don't worry! You can still go and have fun. There are usually refreshments like pizza and soda, and sometimes places other than the dance floor to hang and chat with friends. Offer to sell drinks and snacks if you don't want to have to turn down a dance request.

> "I got on the committee that planned the dances because I just felt more comfortable being involved behind the scenes. At the dance, if my friends were busy, I had things to do like see how the kids were doing collecting tickets, or check to make sure we had enough soda, or talk to the DJ. I was never just standing around not knowing what to do."
> —Victoria

You may want to dance, but feel a bit self-conscious. Totally normal! Practice dancing at home with no one watching. Turn on some music and dance in front of a mirror. You can get some ideas from watching kids move on YouTube. As for slow dances, there's nothing to it: Just put your arms around the boy's waist or his neck (as if you were about to give him a hug) and gently sway back and forth. If you can shift your weight from one foot to the other, you can slow dance!

Sometimes kids will start doing a specific dance like the Macarena or the Electric Slide. If that happens, just jump right in and copy the people around you. The dances are repetitive and easy to learn. Yes, you'll feel a little self-conscious when you first start moving, but when the dance is over, you'll feel better if you tried than if you just stood awkwardly to the side watching everyone else.

> "When my friends and I went to our first middle school dance, we agreed ahead of time to meet at the vending machines every time a slow dance came on. We were just too nervous to deal with that whole thing! Now I'm in my last year of middle school and I have a boyfriend so the slow dances are my faves!"
> —Gabrielle

And remember: Everyone there is much more worried about how he (or she) looks on the dance floor than how you look. The boys are not thinking about how you're moving—they're thinking about how they're moving and whether or not they look lame!

> "The coolest dancers are the girls who just seem like they are having the most fun— laughing and smiling and jumping around waving their hands. You could be the best dancer there but if you're doing your thing in the corner and not smiling, no one cares."
> —Paige

> "Grab a group of friends, head for the sweet spot next to the speakers in front of the DJ and just jump around to the music and have fun! If you're with a few girls in a group laughing and leaping around, that is seriously the best way to have fun at a dance."
> —Amber

Seven Things That Surprised Me About My First School Dance

1. "The music was so loud that it was hard to talk to my friends unless we went into a different room."

2. "It was funny that even during slow songs girls would dance with each other as a joke."

3. "I was surprised that when I requested my favorite song, the DJ actually played it!"

4. "I couldn't believe how hot and thirsty I got! Everybody was so sweaty! I wore a sweater but the next time I'm going to wear a tank top."

5. "The coat room was jammed at the end of the dance! I couldn't find any of my stuff until everyone cleared out. I think at the next dance, when they announce it's the last song, I'll go and get my stuff ahead of everybody else."

6. "It was hard to find my mom at the end because there were a million cars lined up outside. We decided that next time, I'll leave about 15 minutes early so that we can find each other more easily."

7. "Just as many girls ask boys to slow dance as the other way around. You don't have to wait for someone to approach you."

> "Now that I'm in high school, I don't remember who I danced with, but I remember liking to have *someone* to dance with during the slow songs. I do remember standing alone during slow dances and wishing someone had asked me. Or I wish I had been braver and asked someone to dance with me!"
> — Teri

Dance DOs and DON'Ts

DO go to a friend's house before the dance and get ready together. It's more fun that way, and you can give each other tips on what to wear. Maybe you can include a few friends! Major bonus: You'll feel better walking into the dance with a friend or two than by yourself.

DO dress in an outfit that is comfortable, but has a little pizzazz! You might want a little glitter in your hair or shimmery gloss on your lips. The room will probably be dark, but there might be special strobe lights for fun.

DO remind yourself that no one in your grade knows any more about dances and dancing than you do! If you feel a little nervous, you know everyone else does, too! No one really has "dance moves." Just relax and have fun. Grab a group of girls and dance together! You don't need boys in order to have a great time! (Pity the boys—they would feel a little weird dancing with other boys!)

DO go for it and dance with anyone who asks you! After all, it's just 4 minutes of your life. Think of how it would hurt your feelings if you were turned down.

DO request your favorite song from a DJ so you can look forward to dancing with enthusiasm to a song you love! Make sure you don't make these mistakes!

> "I remember asking a really cute guy to dance who said yes and it made my night! Later on a really dorky guy asked me to dance and I said yes and actually had a great time. Maybe that made him feel as happy as I felt when someone said yes to me. One dance with someone doesn't mean you're a couple, whether you'd want that to be the case or not!"
> —Kelsey

Make Sure You DON'T Make These Mistakes

DON'T wear a dress; jeans are more comfortable.

DON'T stand alone in a corner. Even if you are normally shy, try hard to be a social butterfly for the night.

DON'T have a big, heavy dinner right before the dance because you'll feel sick leaping around in a hot, crowded room. Eat a light meal well before the dance. (A lot of times food and drinks will be available at the dance.)

How to Play MASH

Want to predict your future? Where you'll live, what kind of job you'll have, your husband's name? All you need is a piece of paper and a pen! This game is even more fun if you play with a friend.

Write the letters M, A, S, H at the top of the paper. These letters stand for Mansion, Apartment, Shack, and House. (To make it more fun, you can add I and O—MASHIO—which stand for Igloo and Outhouse.)

Now think of a few more categories for predictions. In this example, we'll choose Husband, Job, Number of Kids, and Location (meaning, where you will live). Other categories might be things like Income, Pet, or Hobby. Use your imagination!

For each category, list four items. If you're playing with a friend, you can pick two items and your friend can pick the other two. (Your friend can be as "cruel" as she wants to be! Watch out, or you might end up marrying your grumpy math teacher and living on the bottom of the ocean!).

If you're playing by yourself, you should pick two items that would make for a great future, and two that would be pretty awful! For example, for Husbands, you should list two people you love and two people you can't stand. You can be as silly or serious as you want! For "Location," you can write Paris or the North Pole. For "Jobs," list astronaut… or cupcake taster!

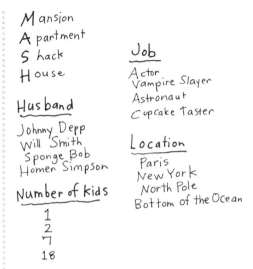

Next, close your eyes as your friend slowly starts drawing a spiral. Say "stop" whenever you want to and draw a line through the middle of the spiral. Count how many times the line touches the spiral. This is your magic number. In this case, the magic number is 5.

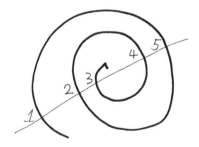

Start from the letter "M" in MASH and begin counting by your magic number (in this case, 5). Go through each item in each row, one by one. Each time you reach the number 5, cross off the item that you land on and start counting

Mansion¹
Apartment²
Shack³
House⁴

Husband

Johnny Depp⁵
Will Smith¹
Sponge Bob²
Homer Simpson³

Number of kids

1 4
2 5
7 ¹
18 ²

Job

Actor ³
Vampire Slayer⁴
Astronaut ⁵
Cupcake Taster¹

Location

Paris ²
New York ³
North Pole ⁴
Bottom of the Ocean ⁵

from 1 again. When you have gone through each category once, start at the beginning of the page and skip over the items that you've crossed off. Keep going until only one item in each category remains.

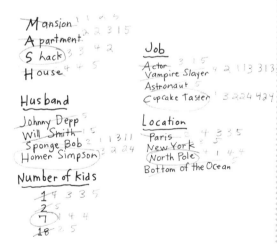

You Can Also Play MASH Online!

Check out these sites:

http://www.scholastic.com/kids/middle-schoolsurvival/mash/

http://www.smartgirl.org/mash.html

http://dollarshort.org/mash/

Mansion¹ ¹
Apartment² ²
Shack³ ³
House⁴ ⁴

Husband

Johnny Depp⁵
Will Smith¹ ⁵
Sponge Bob² ¹
Homer Simpson³ ²

Number of kids

1 4 3
2 5
7 ¹ 4
18 ² 5

Job

Actor ³ ¹
Vampire Slayer⁴ ²
Astronaut ⁵
Cupcake Taster¹ ³

Location

Paris ² 4
New York ³ ⁵
North Pole ⁴ ¹
Bottom of the Ocean ⁵

Now insert the items that remain into this story:

Twenty years from now, you will be happily married to ————(husband). You will live in a charming ————————— (MAS or H) in——————— (location) with your ——— (number) lovely children. You will be a very successful——————— (job) who loves her job.

Fun FAcT

My Dream Date Mad Lib!

Have you ever played Mad Libs? Ask a friend to list the parts of speech below (without showing her the story, of course!). Then insert her answers into the story and read her dream date passage out loud! (If you are playing Mad Libs by yourself, fill out this list of words BEFORE looking at the Mad Lib below. Then, fill in the blanks with the words that you listed below.) Remember, a noun is a person, place, or thing; a verb is an action word; an adjective describes a noun; and an adverb describes an action and usually ends in "ly."

Noun: _____   City: _____

Adjective: _____   Noun: _____

Color: _____   Verb: _____

Adjective: _____   Adverb: _____

Adjective: _____   Noun: _____

Adjective: _____   Plural Noun: _____

My Dream Date

I still haven't met the _____ of my dreams, but I know he is out there somewhere!
                          Noun

He has_____hair and_____eyes: the perfect combination! He is tall,
        Adjective   Color

_____, and handsome, and he has a_____sense of humor. On our first date, he
Adjective   Adjective

will take me to a_____restaurant in_____where we will dine on my
                 Adjective   City

favorite dish:_____ . After, we will_____through the park and he will hold
              Noun   Verb Adverb

my_____ ... how romantic! The next day, he will send me a bouquet of_____
   Noun   Plural Noun

to show how much he cares about me. So sweet!

Ask your friends to take this just-for-fun Dating **Would You Rather Quiz!**

Would You Rather...

...date a guy who takes his puppet with you on a date and talks only through his puppet OR a guy who takes his cat on a leash everywhere the two of you go?

...have your mother sit next to you on a dinner date OR have an allergic reaction to your dinner and immediately break out in hives all over your face?

...date a guy who constantly uses a lint roller to keep his clothes perfectly clean OR a guy who wears the same stained pants five days in a row?

...date a guy who speaks in a weird made-up language that you can barely understand OR one who clears his throat every few seconds?

> "I am part of a really fun group of four best friends. None of us have boyfriends, but we have so much fun doing stuff together that other kids always say that they want to be like us!"
> —Desiree

Secrets of the Single Life

Dating boys can be fun, and having a special guy to call your own can be great, too. But if you are not interested in boys yet, or if you are between boyfriends, being single can be great! Really!

Here's What Being Single Means:

...you don't have to worry about what he's doing when he's not with you
...you don't have to feel guilty about flirting with another boy
...you aren't waiting around for a phone call from him before you make plans with your girlfriends
...you're free to have guy friends with no one feeling jealous about it
...you don't have to deal with the whole break up thing
...you can dance with a different boy for each slow song, not the same boy all night
...you don't have to worry that when you break up, all of his friends will be mad at you
...you don't have to worry about how far are the two of you are going to go
...you don't spend even one second worrying about why he was talking to another girl or why he didn't pick up his cell phone when you called
...when you find a guy worth dating, he won't be one out of 30 past boyfriends, he'll be special

The Secret Meanings of Dreams

Some people believe that dreams hold the key to our secret thoughts and hidden feelings. For many, many years, people have been trying to unlock the mystery of dreams and interpret their meaning. This dream "dictionary" is a good starting point if you are interested in exploring the meaning of your own dreams. (Like your astrological forecast, this is meant for fun. Don't take it too seriously!)

If you dream about **aliens**, this might mean that you are worried about something in your life that is strange or new, or people you've never met.

If you dream about being at an **amusement park**, this might mean that your life is too busy and that you need to take more time out for fun.

If you dream about standing in front of an **audience**, this might mean that you feel people close to you pay a lot of attention to what you do, or it might mean that you are afraid that people will find out your secret thoughts.

If you dream about carrying a heavy **backpack**, this might mean that you feel you are carrying a heavy burden in your life.

If you dream that you are **barefoot**, this might mean that you are a relaxed, happy-go-lucky person.

If you dream that you are at the **beach** looking toward the ocean, this might mean that you are aware of important but unfamiliar changes happening in your life; if you have your back to the ocean, this might mean that you are going toward something comforting and familiar.

If you dream that you are in a **messy bedroom**, this might mean that you are in the middle of a complicated relationship.

If you dream about riding a **bicycle**, this might mean that you need to have a better balance in your life between schoolwork and fun.

If you dream about a **boy** you don't like, this might mean that you secretly like things about him, or that you want to be in love right now.

If you dream that you missed the school **bus**, this might mean that you feel as if your friends are leaving you behind.

If you dream that you are driving a **car**, this might mean that you are very ambitious and you feel confident in your ability to move on to the next stage of life.

If you dream about a **cemetery**, this might mean that you are leaving behind old habits and starting fresh.

If you dream about falling off a **cliff**, this might mean that you feel like you are losing control of a certain situation in your life or that you are worried about starting something new, like a new school year.

If you dream about changing your **clothes**, this might mean that you realize that you need to make some changes to adapt to a new situation.

If you dream about a friendly **dog**, this might mean that you will have good luck with friends and social situations.

If you dream about an **elephant**, this might mean that you will have lots of good luck in the future. (Horses, rabbits, and fish are also lucky in dreams.)

If you dream about an **exam or a test**, this might mean that your loyalty or talents are being questioned or put to the test.

If you dream about a **fire**, this might mean that you are having trouble with a transition, or that you have passionate and strong relationships.

If you dream about **flying**, this might mean that you should have more confidence in yourself and your ability to do whatever you set your mind to. It could also mean that you will soon be free of something that has been bothering you.

If you dream about **garbage**, this might mean that you are ready to toss out bad habits and attitudes and move ahead in a positive way.

If you dream about having blonde or brown **hair**, this might mean that you will be a loyal friend; if you dream about having red hair this might mean that changes are happening in your life. If you have curly hair in your dream, this might mean that a boy will try to come on to you!

If you dream about **kittens**, this might mean trouble in the future, like someone tricking you.

If you dream about walking down a **long hall**, this might mean that you are annoyed about a situation in your life that keeps repeating itself.

If you dream about getting **lost** on your way home, this might mean that you are going through a period where you have lost a little faith in yourself and are a bit insecure.

If you dream about a **ladder**, this might mean that it's a great time to make new friends. It might also mean that you feel you are making progress in some area of your life, one step at a time.

If you dream about being **late** to class, this might mean that you're afraid of change or worried about your future.

If you dream about being **laughed at**, this might mean that you will have good news about money.

If your dream includes things that are **messy**, this might mean that you will soon find an answer to something that is upsetting you.

If you dream about **money**, this might mean that you should pay more attention to those in your family. If you dream about **paying money**, this might mean that you feel that your life is very demanding right now.

If you dream about being **naked** in public (or in your underwear), this might mean that you are worried about people seeing the real you, that you are hiding something from your friends, or that you're afraid of being embarrassed in a social situation.

If you dream about having an **operation**, this might be a sign of good luck; things that have pained you are being healed.

If your dream features a **pencil**, this might mean that one of your relationships won't last, although pencils may also be signs of good luck.

If you dream about a **swimming pool** that is full, this might mean that you will be very happy in your relationships; an empty pool might mean that you are having trouble with your friendships and love life.

If you dream about being in a **race**, this might mean that other people are jealous of the things you've accomplished.

If your dream takes place in a **restaurant**, this might mean that you feel stressed out by all of the choices you must make.

If you are **running** in your dream, this might mean that you feel stuck in a relationship and unable to get out of it.

If you are **sad** in your dream, this might mean that something happy is about to happen!

If you dream that you are in a **shopping mall**, this might mean that everything you need emotionally (as far as friendship and love) is available to you.

If you dream about being **sick**, this might mean that you are in a relationship that is not good for you. (This is also true for dreams about spiders.)

If you dream about throwing **snowballs**, this might mean that you are going to have to deal with an embarrassing situation.

If you dream about climbing **stairs**, this might mean that your social status is about to take a step up.

If your **teacher** appears in a dream, this might mean that you need guidance right now. If you dream that **you are a teacher**, this might mean that there is something you feel you must explain to others.

If you dream about missing a **test**, this might mean that you are concerned that you can't live up to the expectations others have of you. It does not mean that you are likely to miss a test in real life, but that you don't want to let anyone down.

If you dream about being **underwater**, this might mean that you feel overwhelmed by something and need to get control of it.

If you dream that you are **younger**, this might mean that you are frustrated that you haven't been able to correct some of your past mistakes.

Chapter 4

Secrets from the Classroom

In elementary school, you had one classroom and one classroom teacher, a desk that was all yours, and maybe a cubby for your coat and lunchbox. You had a few other teachers for "specials," like P.E., art, and music, but you spent most of your day in one familiar room. When you did go to a "specials" class, your teacher led you there as a group.

In middle school, you may have seven or eight teachers, each with his or her own room, and a class schedule that is different from everyone else's. Your schedule might rotate, with classes that don't meet at the same time every day. You might even have some classes that alternate, meaning that they meet every other day. Yikes!

Now, for the good news… A lot of things will feel very familiar. The basic subjects you take in middle school will be very much like the ones you took in elementary school: English, math, social studies, and science. If you were a math whiz in elementary school, you'll love the challenge of middle school math classes! If you couldn't wait to do science experiments in fourth and fifth grade, you'll probably love them even more in middle school, because you'll be doing more complicated and interesting things in real science labs. You might also have a computers class, a foreign language class, a food prep

"I love having different teachers and classrooms for every subject. You never get bored and the day doesn't drag at all!"
—Olivia

"In middle school, you're older, and the teachers treat you that way. A lot of the kids I know are friends with the younger teachers. It's fun to hang out after school in the cool teachers' classrooms…. Not so much the cranky older teachers, but definitely the younger ones…"
—Natalie

class, or a health class. These will be new subjects for just about everyone, so you'll all be learning together.

Everyone in your grade will also be learning how to follow a class schedule and change rooms just like you are. It's not as if you will be the only one trying to figure things out! Teachers know that it can be confusing at first, and most of them will be very understanding. Once you've had a week or two of following your class schedule, you'll feel much more comfortable. It won't be long before you tape your schedule inside your locker because you don't need to check it all the time to see where you're going. You've got the routine down, no problem!

In Class

You will have a few minutes to get from one class to another. There will be plenty of time if you walk directly to your next class; probably not enough time to make weekend plans with your three best friends in the hallway. You may also need to stop at your locker between classes to pick up a book or notebook.

> "I try to look at the teachers when they are talking so that they know I'm listening. One time I had to give a report in front of the class and half of the kids were looking down or talking to each other and it made me feel awful!"
> —Becca

> "There's a fine line as far as when to walk into the classroom. You basically want to walk in just before the bell rings. That way, it's clear you've been socializing (instead of just sitting there waiting for class to start) but you don't get in trouble with the teacher."
> —Tanya

> "You should always organize your binder exactly the way the teacher tells you to. It makes it a lot easier if you have to look something up and you'll get a better grade on your notebook check."
> —Eyda

Your teachers will expect you to arrive on the first day with a notebook and pen for taking some notes, but they will hand out a list of specific supplies you'll need to buy for that class. Teachers often want students to have a binder of a certain size, lined paper, dividers for keeping notes organized, pens, and pencils. They may also want you to have a calculator, dictionary, ruler, or graph paper. When you get the lists from all of your teachers, ask your mom or dad to take you to the store as soon as possible because every middle school student will be looking for the very same supplies you need!

If you haven't already, you'll learn to take notes as the teacher lectures in front of the class. You'll use your notes to study for tests, so they need to capture the most important things that the teacher says. You can't write down every word, so you need to understand the basic theme of the day's lecture. Once you have figured out the most important ideas that the teacher will be discussing, you'll know what to jot down The theme will often be clear from the reading assignment the night before. Not sure what the teacher will be talking about? You can always get to class early and ask.

Note Taking DOs and DON'Ts

Follow these tips for taking good, clear notes!

DO start every class by turning to a new page in your notebook. Write the date at the top of the page. Also write down the topic of the day if you know it.

DO listen for key words that tell you something important is coming up. The teacher may be very clear and say, "This is important." He may number his points: "There are three reasons this battle was significant. First…" He may use words like "major point," "basic idea," "critical concept," or give another side of the story and say "in contrast to that…" When he says, "In conclusion" or something that means he is summarizing the day's lecture, be sure to write that down.

DO underline the important ideas right as you jot them down.

DO draw charts or diagrams in your notes if that helps you to remember or understand an idea.

DO go through your notes later that day and highlight the parts that are the most important. That will help when you are studying for tests.

Make Sure You DON'T Make These Mistakes!

DON'T write notes on small pieces of paper with the idea of copying them into a notebook "later."

DON'T squeeze lots of words onto a page. You want to leave room so that you can go back and add things later.

DON'T scribble. You may think that you'll remember what that scribble means when you're studying for the next test, but it's more likely that you won't!

DON'T wait until the day of a test to ask the teacher about something he talked about in class. If you don't understand your notes, talk to the teacher after class and ask him to explain it. Or better yet, raise your hand in class and ask a question the moment something seems confusing or unclear to you.

Speed Up Your Note Taking with These Abbreviations!

b/c – because
w/ – with
w/o – without
eg – for example
= – is the same as
+ – and
~ – approximately

If you miss a day of school (or are late and miss a class), you are responsible for making up the work. School policies vary, but you'll want to make time to visit every teacher after school on the day you return to find out what you missed and what they would like you to do.

Homework

Yes, yes, you will have more homework. It's a bummer, but it's just a fact of middle school life. Still, homework is not just something teachers give you randomly to keep you from watching TV or checking your MySpace. There is meaning behind those assignments!

Some of your homework is to get you ready for class the next day. Maybe you'll read chapters in a book that you will be talking about, or you will research a science topic for an experiment you'll be doing. You will feel a lot more confident going into a class when you've done the **preparation work** the teacher asked you to do.

Practice homework is assigned so that you can get a concept down perfectly before moving on to the next one. There isn't enough time in class for you to practice something again and again; that's why this part is done at home. A lot of math homework is assigned so that you can perfect a concept and be ready to move ahead.

When you study for a test or write a report, you are doing something called **performance homework**. This lets the

Idea!

Some teachers have a master notebook in the front of the room. Students take turns photocopying their notes for the day and putting them into the master notebook. That way, if someone is absent, she can go to the notebook and find out exactly what she missed.

Top Tip

Keep a folder at home for each class. When you get a test or a paper returned to you, put it in the folder. Teachers aren't perfect, and sometimes they make mistakes. If there is a question about whether or not you turned in an assignment or what grade you got, you need to be able to show a teacher your work. (These materials will help when you are getting ready for a final test, too.) You also might want to have a general folder for permission slips, yearbook info, and things that aren't specific to one class.

teacher know that you understand what she's taught you and can put it to use.

It may sound like commonsense advice, but you'll want to do your homework neatly, without a lot of crossed out words and messy smudges. Read your work over carefully before you turn it in to make sure there are no mistakes. And perhaps the most important thing you can do is to turn in your homework on time. Some teachers won't accept late homework at all, and most of them will take points off of your grade for late assignments. They are trying to prepare you for high school and college, where you will have to meet lots of deadlines.

Use your study halls wisely! Don't use them to bang out homework that's due the next period; use them to start homework due the next day. That way, if you have questions, you can talk to the teacher before you go home.

What Is Plagiarism?

Plagiarism is when a person steals someone else's words or ideas and pretends they are her own. This can mean copying and pasting information from a website, copying something from a book, or even from a friend. If you pretend that you wrote something when you really didn't, this is called plagiarism. If you use someone else's words, you need to put quotation marks around them and give the author credit. (By the way, there are lots of ways teachers can tell if you've plagiarized, so it's just not worth the risk!)

"A bunch of us walk to the public library every day after school. We always sit at the same table and do our homework together—and quietly gossip about what happened at school that day, of course!"

—Sadie

"I follow the same routine everyday: after-school snack, homework, dinner, practice flute, finish homework, then TV or something fun. I don't even think about it, I just do it. That way I'm not tempted by other stuff."

—Brie

How Can I Possibly Get All of My Homework Done?!

1 Write a schedule for yourself showing what time you plan to do your homework and then stick to it! List the most urgent things first, like a paper that is due the next day.

2 Plan to work when you are most productive, like after school or right after dinner.

3 Focus when you are doing your homework. If you have the TV on in the background, you will have a hard time paying attention to your work and it will not only take longer but it won't be done as well.

4 Set up a place to do homework with no distractions, good light, and plenty of space to spread out your books and other things you need.

Top Tip

Before you go to bed, check to make sure all your homework is done and packed up in your backpack for the next day. If you wait until morning to toss things in your backpack, you're more likely to forget something.

"At school we have HABs, homework assignment books. I don't know what I would do without mine! I write down every assignment because by the end of the day, I kind of forget what happened in my first class!"

—Johanna

"I always try to take a big project that feels overwhelming and break it up into smaller pieces that don't freak me out as much. Like if I have a big project due on France, I'll mark down on my calendar which day I'll go to the library and get books, which day I'll do the poster, and which day I'll write the paper."

—Yasmin

Toss It or Keep It?

Here is a guideline for knowing what to throw away and what to hang on to...

Toss it
- Info about a field trip that has already happened
- First drafts of papers (as long as you keep the final draft)
- Instructions for homework assignments and projects

Keep it until the end of the year
- All graded assignments
- Info about how grades are determined in each class
- Study guides that you made for quizzes (they'll come in handy when you need to review for the test in that subject!)

Keep it forever (or at least for a few years)
- The test or paper with the wonderful comment from your teacher
- Notebooks that you might refer to when you are taking an advanced class in that subject next year
- Report cards
- Certificates of recognition and awards
- School photos

> "I plan my time better during softball season. I have less free time, so I tend to really crack down and get stuff done."
> —Jen

My Daily Schedule

Every day, make yourself a schedule with time slots for every half hour from the time you get up in the morning to the time you go to bed at night. Then fill it in, beginning with the things that you must do at certain times, like school or piano lessons. Block out dinnertime, also. Then begin to fill in the blanks with things like homework and chores (and even a favorite TV show). Some days, like Saturdays, you will list more social activities with friends than, say, Mondays. Make sure that you are realistic about homework assignments: If a project will take three hours, don't try to squeeze it into two. You'll just get frustrated if you have to start moving things around on your schedule. If you have a long-term assignment, spread it out over several days or weeks. If you have a book that must be read by the end of the month, for instance, write down the number of pages you must read every night in order to meet the deadline.

> "I have a big monthly calendar that takes up my entire desk. I do my work on top of it. I mark off things like when reports are due, when my band concerts are, and things like that so I can look down and see what's coming up. I also mark when I need to start studying for a big chapter test."
> — Sarah

Stuff I HAVE to Do Today:

Chores at home:

_____

_____

_____

Homework:

_____

_____

_____

_____

Other commitments:

_____

_____

Stuff I WANT to Do Today:

Activities:

_____

_____

Social life:

_____

_____

Other things:

_____

_____

The **most important things** on my list today are...

_____

_____

When those things are done, **THEN** I can...

_____

_____

7:00 a.m. _____	2:30 p.m. _____
7:30 a.m. _____	3:00 p.m. _____
8:00 a.m. _____	3:30 p.m. _____
8:30 a.m. _____	4:00 p.m. _____
9:00 a.m. _____	4:30 p.m. _____
9:30 a.m. _____	5:00 p.m. _____
10:00 a.m. _____	5:30 p.m. _____
10:30 a.m. _____	6:00 p.m. _____
11:00 a.m. _____	6:30 p.m. _____
11:30 a.m. _____	7:00 p.m. _____
12:00 noon _____	7:30 p.m. _____
	8:00 p.m. _____
12:30 p.m. _____	8:30 p.m. _____
1:00 p.m. _____	9:00 p.m. _____
1:30 p.m. _____	9:30 p.m. _____
2:00 p.m. _____	10:00 p.m. _____

Book and Binder Covers

Your first assignment in middle school will probably be to cover your books. You can use stretchy book socks that you'll find in office supply and department stores, or you can make your own. It can be fun to make your own unique book covers!

When you shop at stores like Guess, American Eagle, or Abercrombie, be sure to save the cool shopping bags! (You can also use decorative gift bags.)

Use those to cover your books so that you can carry them by the handles, as shown above.

You can also use paper grocery bags to cover your books. Get your friends to sign their names and write messages to you, or jot down favorite song lyrics and quotes. You can also use rubber stamps to make designs. If you use stickers or glue on cut-outs, you can use clear contact paper to protect your design.

When you buy binders, get the ones with the clear plastic covers so that you can slip a sheet of paper behind the plastic to personalize it. (If you already have binders that don't have plastic covers, you can decoupage a photo collage on the front or cover your collage with clear contact paper.)

Make a collage using words cut out of magazines and photos of your friends, favorite celebrities, your pets... anything important to you! Anyone who looks at

your binder will know lots about you with just a glance!

Help! My Teacher Doesn't Like Me!

Thankfully, most teachers are terrific people who went into teaching because they truly love helping kids learn. Now and again, though, a not-so-terrific one slips in. Maybe you have one of those, and you feel like she's not grading you fairly or being as nice to you as she should be.

> "Don't listen to what other kids say about a certain teacher. Try to go in with an open mind. In sixth grade, everyone said I would hate this teacher, Mrs. Brown, but I actually really liked her. She was hard but fair, and she kept the bad kids in line."
> —Dana

Talk to your friends after class to try to figure out whether the teacher is just an unhappy person who is nasty to everyone or whether she's singling you out and treating you unfairly. If she is treating everyone badly, she's either a grumpy person or a teacher who is insecure and thinks that the only way to keep kids in line is to be mean. (Or she has something happening in her personal life that is making it hard for her to teach.)

Talking to the Teacher

In elementary school, your mom or dad probably spoke to the teacher for you if there was an issue at school. But now that you're in middle school, you should try talking to the teacher yourself first. It's not hard if you plan ahead.

Ask yourself: What is my goal? What do I hope will happen after my conversation? Do I want a different grade on a paper? Do I want a few extra days to work on my project? Having a clear goal in mind will help you develop a strategy and get what you want.

If you have a problem, see if you can offer a solution also. ("I know I chose Martinique for my project, but I'm having trouble finding information about that country. I realized that there is a lot more on Haiti. Would it be all right if I changed the topic of my paper to Haiti?")

Approach your teacher at a time that is convenient for her. You may want to make an appointment. Teachers are much more relaxed after school, especially when you can talk one-on-one. You're more likely to achieve your goal if you choose your time wisely.

In that case, you'll just have to figure out how to work with her. Try to identify what really annoys her (talking in class, turning homework in late…) and avoid doing those things. Always act in a pleasant way. She is in charge, after all. Ask yourself, what do you want from her? Chances are, you want to learn the info and get the grade you deserve. So you need to focus on making that happen. On the plus side, the experience will help you learn how to deal with a difficult person. Someday, you may have an uncooperative boss or roommate and you'll know how to handle her thanks to your experience with a tough teacher. At least in middle school, you only have the teacher for one class, not the whole day like in elementary school.

> **"I had an English teacher who was super strict and not nice at all. One day, I left my sweatshirt in her classroom and I went to get it after school. She was so much nicer to me after school than she normally was in class! We actually chatted for about 10 minutes! I told my mom about it and she said that it was probably because she was a new teacher and she thought she had to act tough so that the kids would behave."**
> —Shannon

> **"My math teacher yelled a lot and acted like he didn't like me. One day, when I was feeling super brave, I went to him after class and asked him if I had done anything to upset him. I told him that I'd like to apologize if I did and maybe start over. He seemed really surprised and said my class had a couple of tough kids in it and he felt like he needed to keep them in line, but that I was doing great! He was much nicer to me after that."**
> —Yolanda

If you truly feel that your teacher is being nasty just to you, you need to ask yourself some tough questions. First of all, are you doing anything that is making her angry? Second, do you tend to have your feelings hurt a lot more easily than other kids?

If you believe that you aren't doing anything wrong and you aren't overly sensitive, then you have two choices. You can have your parents come to school and help you work it out, or you can do your best to deal with the situation yourself by speaking to the teacher or by trying to do things that will improve the relationship. If the situation is so upsetting to you that it's affecting the rest of your day, your parents need to intervene. They can ask that you be moved into a different class.

Of course, if a teacher ever does anything physical, uses bad language, or calls you names, you definitely need to talk to an adult who will take action. No matter what course of action you decide to take, make notes of the times when you feel you were treated unfairly so that you can talk in specifics, and not just make general accusations, like, "She's mean to me."

Remember: The relationship with this teacher will end when school does. You never have to have her again. Feel sorry for her kids or her husband or anyone who has to deal with her forever!

Fun FAcT

In an online poll by pbskids.org, kids answered a question about what they would do if they felt like a teacher didn't like them. Forty-one percent would talk to a parent, 31 percent would keep it inside and try hard to do well in the class, and 27 percent admitted that they would play pranks on the teacher to get revenge!

"I did not like my science teacher at all. One day, I borrowed his favorite pen and forgot to return it. He thought he lost it. When I 'found' it and returned it to him, I was a huge hero and then he loved me. So then I started to like him a little bit more, too."
—Charlotte

Detention: Yikes!

If you get a detention, don't panic. Serving a detention in a teacher's room after school is not as serious as serving one in the principal's office or in a special detention room. Apologize to the teacher in person or in writing for the behavior that got you in trouble, even if it seems like the rule you broke wasn't that serious (like chewing gum or wearing a coat in class). After all, rules are rules and they apply to everyone. Never skip a detention: That will make the situation much worse. Just promise yourself (and your parents) that you will try your hardest to follow the rules for the rest of the year.

"You can raise your hand in class and do well on tests and still have the respect of the other kids. Don't be embarrassed about being a good student (but don't be all braggy either)!"
—Latiesha

Secrets to Surviving a Group Project

1 Appoint the most organized one in the group to be the project leader.

2 Divide up the work load equally. Write down who will be doing what and the deadlines for different tasks, and make a copy for each person. Everyone is good at something, so make sure that kids are assigned tasks they feel confident tackling.

3 Make sure everyone has a chance to express thoughts and ideas so that every member of the group feels like an important part of the project.

4 If you notice that one member of the group is slacking off, don't wait until the day before the project is due to talk to him. Address the situation early on, and in a positive way. Ask if he would like to switch assignments with someone else, or if he needs help getting started. Find a way to compliment him ("Your idea for the poster was great!") and hopefully he will feel motivated to get to work. If he still can't seem to get his act together, don't feel bad about mentioning something to your teacher. It isn't fair for your grade to suffer because of a lazy group member!

Suggest These Ideas for Fun Things to Do at School!

Say "cheese" day: For $5 a photo (given to the yearbook committee), kids can have pics taken with their friends that are *guaranteed* to go in the yearbook. (With five friends in a photo, that's just $1 each!)

Pay a dollar, wear a hat day: To earn money for a school project or charity, kids can pay a dollar each for the privilege of wearing their favorite hats to school.

Field-trip Fridays: Kids who get good grades and do good deeds are awarded coupons by teachers that can be redeemed for monthly field trips to fun places.

Dress-down day: Kids who normally wear uniforms to school get one day a year to wear anything that they want to (within reason, of course!).

Quizzes and Tests

Is the answer A, B, or C? True or false? Was my first answer right or should I go with my second thought? AAAHHH!

No one likes taking tests. But that's the method most teachers use to determine whether or not their students have learned the material, so tests are unavoidable. Most kids feel a lot of pressure when they take tests. They put pressure on themselves to do well, and they feel pressure from their teachers and parents, too. They might even compete with friends for the best grades!

There are strategies you can use to make taking tests a little less stressful. Here's what some middle schoolers advise:

"First thing, write down your name on the test. I've screwed that up before."

"I always get to class a little early on the day of a test so that I have time to get out my pencils, stash my backpack, and just chill for a second. I hate rushing in as the teacher is handing out the test papers."

"Wear a watch or at least make sure you can see a clock. There's nothing worse than running out of time before you finish, especially if you know you could have gotten all the questions right with enough time to answer them!"

"For tests, I try to sit in the front row near the teacher's desk. I don't need some kid in the back who is tapping his pencil or talking to himself to drive me crazy! I also don't want to sit in back with the kids who cheat."

"A couple of days before a big test, I stay after school and ask the teacher to go over anything I'm not really sure about. It makes me feel more confident and I also figure it lets the teacher know I really care what grade I get on it."

"Focus on your own test and don't let yourself get distracted. It can really freak you out when you're only halfway done with a page and the kid next to you turns to the next page! I mean, maybe he only answered half the questions, but you won't know that and it will just upset you!"

"I make myself read the directions twice. I messed up one time because I kind of skimmed them and didn't answer the questions the right way. So now I make sure I take the time to figure out what I'm supposed to do."

"I remind myself that there will be a lot of grades in the class, and probably extra credit stuff I could do, and that this test is only one grade, so it's not like my life depends on acing it."

"I skip the questions I don't know and save those for last. I make sure I give great answers for the ones I know, then go back and try to figure out the other ones. If I'm not sure of the answer, I guess. I never leave something blank because then I *know* it's wrong!"

"I like studying right before I go to bed, and then reviewing what I studied as soon as I wake up in the morning. I feel like the information really sinks into my brain as I sleep!"
—Alexis

"I'm a swimmer, and I know that being able to make myself relax and stay calm is critical to winning a race. I tell myself the same thing on test day."

"It's important to figure out how fast you need to work. I try to pace myself so that I have time to go back through one final time and check my answers. It's also good to know which teachers will let you come after school and finish the test and which ones never would."

"Eat a really good breakfast and lunch on test days!"

"If you are a little nervous, you're actually more alert and you might do better than if you were totally chill."

"My biggest piece of advice is to take the whole period to do the test, even if you finish early. Go back and check your work and see if you can add anything to essay questions. Even if you can add a couple of points, that could be the difference between a B+ and an A-!"

"Usually it's not a good idea to ask kids who already took the test if it was easy or hard. You might get too relaxed or too anxious depending on what they say and end up not doing your best."

"Don't try to learn everything the night before the test because that makes you more nervous. Study each night over the course of a few days so that you have confidence that you know the stuff that will be on it."

Five Test-taking Tips

1 Keep up with the regular class work so that you don't have to play catch-up right before a test. The minute you don't understand something, go after class or after school and ask the teacher to explain it. You can even get a tutor to help if you need it.

2 To study for a major test, look through your quizzes to see where you had some trouble and might need to focus a little more attention.

3 Ask some of the better students in the class if they would like to form a study group. You can get together a few days before a big test and quiz each other.

4 Make sure you find out everything you can about the test. Ask the teacher exactly what material will be covered and what format the test will be (multiple choice, essay, fill-in-the-blank…). Also find out what you are allowed to have with you on test day: Can you have a calculator? Is it an "open notebook" test?

5 Make flashcards and ask your mom, dad, or older sibling to quiz you.

"I hate being asked about my grades! If I did too well, other kids get mad at me! And if I didn't do that well, I'm embarrassed to say. So now if someone asks, I just say, 'I'm happy with the way I did' or 'It was hard but I did my best' or something vague like that. Sometimes I even just say, 'Good!' and leave it at that!"
—Kate

"I love what my social studies teacher always says before a test. He goes, 'The results of this test do not reflect your worth as a person and will not change the direction of the rest of your life. So relax and do your best.'"
—Jessie

Secret for Memorizing Dates

Will you always remember 1492 as the date that Columbus sailed the ocean blue? Rhymes like that one are the secret to remembering dates! Come up with a little rhyme that creates a picture in your head. For instance, the German battleship Bismarck sank in 1941. Remember this by picturing battleship guns going underwater: 1941, guns all done. The sillier the rhyme, the more likely you are to remember it!

What Is Cheating?

Cheating is when you write down answers to a test ahead of time and then copy them onto the test paper.

Cheating is when you copy answers off of another student's paper (or let him copy answers off of your paper).

Cheating is when you say that something is your own work, when it is really someone else's work.

Cheating is when you do someone else's work for him.

Cheating is when you break school rules about class work and homework.

"I knew this girl who cheated all the time in math class. She got better grades than me and it really bugged me. But as the year went on, she had trouble understanding what we were doing in class because she had never really learned the stuff that came before it. I don't know how she is going to do math next year."
—Shavon

"A real friend doesn't ask you to help them cheat on stuff."
—Brooke

"I cheated on a quiz one time. I wrote down some answers on my wrist. I got an A. But I've never felt so bad about a grade in my whole life. I never even showed the quiz to my mom. I felt so guilty that it totally wasn't worth it."
— Ali

Grades

You are graded to show how well you have learned the material in each of your classes. Report cards often come out every quarter, or four times in a school year. Some schools send progress reports home a few weeks before report cards so that students have a chance to improve their grades before the final grades are submitted. Some schools also allow parents and students to go online and review all of the grades given out by each teacher. This is very helpful for students who want to make sure they have not missed an assignment or who want to see where their strengths and weaknesses are.

Your grades are usually a combination of several things: your test and quiz grades, homework assignments (including projects and papers), class work such as labs or worksheets, notebook checks, and class participation (which includes attendance and behavior). At the beginning of the year, each teacher should tell you how she determines your grade. For some teachers, tests might have the most weight. For others, like foreign language teachers, class participation might be as important as quizzes. Make sure you know what each teacher expects of you. You'll also

want to find out how letter grades are assigned. In some schools, an average of 90 to 100 is an "A," while for others, the "A" range might be 93 to 100. It is important to get the best grades you can. You will feel better about your time in school if you know you are doing your best work. In some classes this might be an "A" and in other classes, it might mean a lower grade. If you feel that your teachers or parents have unrealistic expectations as far as the grades you should be getting, have an honest talk with them. The adults in your life just want you to be successful. They wouldn't, however, want to put an unreasonable amount of stress on you. By talking things over, you can determine together what your goals should be in each class.

Lighten Up!

Does your backpack feel like it's full of bricks? Ugh! Some schools provide two sets of textbooks, one for school and one for home, and others offer a lot of information online, eliminating the need for hauling heavy books around. Until your school addresses the problem of too-heavy backpacks, here are some tips:

• Buy a backpack that is not overly large, with padded shoulder straps and a waist belt to distribute the load. You'll want one with lots of compartments so that the weight is distributed more evenly.

• Pack it with the heaviest books closest to your back.

• To pick it up without hurting your back, place your full backpack on a table. Back into it, bend your knees a little, then pull the straps over your shoulders and fasten the waist belt.

• Don't wear it slung over one shoulder. That can cause back pain.

Fun FAcT

According to pediatricians, full backpacks should weigh less than 15 percent of a child's body weight. More than half of children surveyed recently carry backpacks that are too heavy for their weight.

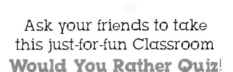

Ask your friends to take this just-for-fun Classroom **Would You Rather Quiz**!

At School, Would You Rather...

...say something terrible about your English teacher and find out she is standing right behind you OR stand up in front of your English class to recite a poem and forget the entire thing?

...walk in to class and realize that you forgot to study for a huge test OR make a bathroom stop on the way to class and get locked in, missing the test entirely?

...hand in a homework assignment, only to realize that you wrote a personal note to your BFF on the back OR fall asleep in class and start talking in your sleep?

...have to do a group project with your arch enemy OR miss out on your crush's awesome birthday bash because you have to work on a big project that you put off until the last minute?

...accidentally give your crush the wrong info on a homework assignment, causing him to get a bad grade OR have to give an embarrassing oral report on puberty in front of your entire class?

HOT OR NOT?

What's hot: A side pocket on your backpack that can fit your Nalgene or Sigg water bottle
What's not: A million little key chains and other dangly things hanging off of the zippers on your backpack

What's hot: Doing a really cool extra credit assignment to bring up your grade
What's not: Sucking up to a teacher just to bring up your grade

What's hot: Carrying a few books in your arms to lighten the load in your backpack
What's not: A backpack that rolls on wheels (too hard to get up and down the stairs and too likely to trip someone!)

What's hot: Sharing class notes with a friend who was absent from school
What's not: Sharing information about a test with your friend who was absent from school (and will be taking the test a different day)

"I joined the cross-country running team because I wanted to get into better shape. I'm one of the slowest ones on the team. That kind of sucks. But, I'm one of the fastest kids in my gym class now because I run everyday! A lot of times, the teacher asks me to lead the warm-up run because she knows I'm on the team!"
—BriAnna

Secrets to Surviving Gym Class

You've had gym class before, but you probably haven't had to change your clothes before class or shower afterward. This part is awkward for *everyone*, so don't feel as if you're the only one who is a little embarrassed by it. (Remember: No one is looking at you; everyone else is trying to figure out how to keep the others from looking at them!) It won't be long before you (and the other girls new to middle school) will figure out what you can wear on gym day for a quick, simple change and how to clean up easily afterward.

Here are some secrets from girls already in middle school:

• Bring in clean clothes before taking home your dirty ones. (If you take your dirty ones home first, you might forget to bring in a clean set.)

• Always lock your gym locker. For some reason, theft seems to be a big issue in many school locker rooms. Don't ever leave your items sitting on a bench, and don't leave anything too important or expensive in the locker room.

• On gym days, do your hair in a ponytail (or in another style that won't be ruined by sweating and running in class).

• Don't worry if you're not a jock. Most PE teachers don't grade based on how athletic you are. You will get a good grade if you always have gym clothes and sneakers, are dressed and ready for class on time, have a good attitude and try hard, and don't goof around with your friends.

• Always praise other kids around you for their effort. That helps establish a positive feeling in the class.

• Be a good sport and try your hardest. The other kids in the class will respect you for that. After all, the best basketball player in your gym class may need some patience when she doesn't understand a concept in pre-algebra.

• If you wear makeup, bring some extra supplies to school on gym days so that you can touch up after class.

• If you know what sport is coming up in gym class, see if you can get a sibling or friend to practice with you a little. Maybe you can shoot some hoops at the park, practice kicking a soccer ball, or hit a volleyball back and forth for an hour or so. This will give you a bit more confidence.

Check out this site for more gym class survival tips: http://www. beaconstreetgirls.com/avery/ sports/surviving-gym-class

Musical Notes

If you like music, being part of a band or an orchestra can be lots of fun. It's also a nice break from the more academic subjects. If you haven't already started taking lessons on a particular instrument, maybe you can meet with the music teacher or band director and ask for suggestions. Often, a school has instruments to loan out, or the school participates in a program that allows students to rent an instrument inexpensively. Sometimes the director needs students to play certain instruments; if you play a more unusual instrument (maybe the piccolo instead of the flute? The oboe instead of the clarinet?), you'll be more likely to be chosen for special honor bands or jazz bands.

Great Websites for Girls!

Check out these sites to find out what other middle school girls are up to!

Most Helpful Website

http://www.girlslife.com

This website not only provides lots of great information, but it doubles as the perfect way to connect with middle school girls all over the world! Check out the Advice and Girl Talk sections of the site. You can ask questions, read about what's on the minds of other girls your age, and even give advice to girls by leaving comments. Just make sure to ask your mom or dad before you create a user profile on the site. (By the way, you may also want to check out the monthly *Girl's Life* magazine!)

Most Fun All-in-One Website

www.middleschoolsurvival.com

Click on the locker to open up a world of advice, quizzes, games, tips, embarrassing moments (that you can rate!), and other fun stuff for middle school girls! You can even create-a-crush and play MASH on this website!

Most Fictional Fun Website

http://www.beaconstreetgirls.com

This cool site features games and offers advice, ideas, and tips from real middle school girls *and* from fictional BFFs Avery, Isabel, Charlotte, Katani, and Maeve. (You'll have fun figuring out which girl is most like you!) Even if you haven't read *The Beacon Street Girls* series, you can still get to know these five very different girls by reading their blogs and diaries, taking their quizzes, learning from their tips, or taking their advice. You can also create your own locker (similar to a user profile on the website) and join in the fun! Post questions, offer suggestions of your own, hang out in the Beacon Street Girls' town… the website

offers loads of options! (And you can even download the first *Beacon Street Girls* book for free on this website to find out how these five girls survive middle school.)

Most Interesting Survey Website

http://www.smartgirl.org

What a great site for girls who enjoy reading and writing book and movie reviews, checking out original written work by other girls, peeking at other kids' love letters, and voicing their opinions on The Soap Box page! Most of all, you'll love looking at the survey results on topics ranging from siblings to smoking! Do you agree with other middle school girls across the country?

Most Informative Website

http://pbskids.org/itsmylife

You'll have to share this site with the boys, but you'll find all sort of helpful information about studying for tests, managing your time, handling sibling rivalry, being home alone, making money, and many other topics of interest! You'll also read loads of comments from kids all over the world on every subject!

Most Fun "Mixed Bag" Website:

http://www.kidzworld.com

There's something for everyone on this site! Even though boys check out this site, too, you can find great info about such varied topics as your period, yoga moves, pimples, edible jewelry, and the Miss America Pageant! You can also watch movie trailers, keep up with the sports world, and check out cool new toys. Worth checking out!

Chapter 5

Secrets About Parents and Life at Home

Are you wondering why you need to know secrets about parents and home life? After all, you're changing schools, not *families*! What new info could there possibly be?

During the middle school years, it can be tricky to balance your home life with your expanding social life. You need and deserve a bit more independence, but you also need to stay connected to your family.

As you begin to participate in activities that don't involve your family, you may notice that your relationship with your parents becomes strained. You feel as if you are mature enough to make a lot of your own decisions and yet it seems as if your parents are treating you like a child. Sometimes you think they are too intrusive, asking questions about your new friends, what you're doing on the Internet, and what you're saying in a text message.

It may be annoying, but your 'rents are just concerned about your safety and well-being. It may help them relax and cut you more slack if you share as much as you can with them about your friends, schoolwork, and activities. When parents feel left out and uninformed, they tend to worry and feel the need to pry. So tell them how your classes are going and share news about what your friends are up to.

Let them in as much as you can, and you may find that they give you a bit more freedom.

You'll also have to earn your parents' trust. The way to do that is to be truthful with them, and to make good choices when you are with your friends. If they feel you are dependable, honest, and likely to make mature decisions, you will find that they will be less inclined to act like "helicopter parents" who hover, wanting to know every detail of your life.

Reassure them, too, that even though your friends and activities are important, so are they. Make time for household chores, family dinners, and other family activities so that your bond stays strong.

And here's a secret you should know: There will be many times in middle school when you'll be very glad to have parents who care and want to be involved in your life. Your BFFs and boyfriends may change, but your family is always there for you. Home can be a nice escape from the ups and downs of middle school relationships and a comforting place when you want a break from the stresses of school.

Fun Stuff to do with the Fam

Now that you're a little older, are you having trouble coming up with ideas for family fun? Does it seem that everything your parents suggest is a little… uh, *young* for you? Here's a list of suggestions for family time that will be fun for everyone:

Have a video game night! Play Rock Band, Buzz! The Hollywood Quiz, or Scene It? Lights, Camera, Action, all favorites of pre-teens and teens. (Suggest to your parents that the one who wins the most games should be allowed to have a sleepover the next Friday night!)

Embark on a mall scavenger hunt! Combine two fun things for a great family afternoon: the mall and a scavenger hunt! Your list for the hunt can include such things as a penny found face-up, a compliment from a store clerk, a packet of sugar with the name of a restaurant on it, and a shopping bag that has red letters on it.

Play a great board game together! Try Pictionary, SET, Slamwich, or Scrabble! (How about an hour added to Saturday night curfew or an extra hour of TV as the grand prize on game night?)

Volunteer together in your community! Work a shift at your local Community Kitchen, offer to usher at an area theater (and then see the show for free!), or walk dogs at the humane society. There are lots of great volunteer opportunities for families.

Play poker or other cool card games! Check out www.pagat.com to read about the rules and descriptions of loads of fun card games. Use pennies, chocolate coins, or Skittles as poker chips!

> "Even in middle school, I loved to play with my dollhouse but I was embarrassed to tell anyone so I always hid it when friends came over. One time a friend surprised me and dropped in and I was mortified but she was all excited because she said she still played with her dolls sometimes, too."
>
> —Casey

Cook for the family! See if you can vary your family's ho-hum menu by making an ethnic or vegetarian recipe for everyone to try. If you love to read *and* cook, check out this list of cookbooks based on great literature: http://comminfo.rutgers.edu/professionaldevelopment/childlit/ChildrenLit/cookbooks.html.

Fun FAcT

In a recent YMCA poll, 21 percent of teens listed "not having enough time together with parents" as their most significant concern!

HOT OR NOT?

What's hot: Having your own money
What's not: Taking money from your parents in front of your friends

What's hot: Texting your mom and filling her in after the drama club try-outs
What's not: Calling your mom in tears every time something doesn't go perfectly

What's hot: Dinner with the family
What's not: Skipping dinner to chat on the phone with your crush

What's hot: A calendar for noting assignments; a pencil holder for pens, highlighters, and pencils; and your favorite quote taped above your desk
What's not: A box of crayons, safety scissors, and Polly Pockets lined up on your desk

> "I'm jealous of my little sister because she still gets to be a kid, with no real worries. She doesn't have much homework and she can just play. My parents take care of all of her problems."
>
> —Ellen

Home Alone

The older you get, the more likely it is that your parents will leave you home alone, and for longer periods of time. This may be after school or at night. Some girls love the quiet, private time at home; others are a little anxious about being home alone.

There are a few things you can ask your parents to do to make you feel more secure. If you are coming home from school to an empty house, you should have a plan to check in with a parent at a certain time. And your parents should tell you how to reach them at any time if you have an emergency. You'll also want to have the number of a neighbor who is likely to be at home so that you can call her if you need to. Ask your mom or dad to make sure the smoke alarms are working, and to show you where the fire extinguisher is and how to use it. If you don't already have it, you'll want to get caller ID on your phone so that you know whether or not to pick up when you're home alone. If at all possible, have your mom or dad install a peephole in the front door so that you can see who is ringing the bell without opening the door (or just peer out the nearest window to see who's there).

To avoid any problems with your folks, make sure you are in agreement as to what the rules are. Are you allowed to have friends over? Are there any friends you're *not* allowed to have over? Are there rules about television and computer time that you are expected to follow? What are the rules about cooking and the kitchen? Ask your parents to be clear about their expectations. They should write down the house rules so that the whole family knows what they are.

If you are taking care of a sibling when your parents are gone, you'll need to make sure that your parents go over the house rules in front of you both. That way, it will be easier for you to lay down the law if you need to.

Fun FAcT

About one in every ten kids between the ages of 5 and 11 has spent time at home alone. (That means that 9 out of 10 kids have not!)

Home Alone Quiz

How well do you know the rules for staying home by yourself? Answer the following true or false questions and then see how your responses compare to what the experts say.

1 TRUE OR FALSE? Turn up the volume on the TV so that the loud noise will scare off potential intruders.

2 TRUE OR FALSE? You should have access to the family's guns in case you need to defend yourself.

3 TRUE OR FALSE? You shouldn't tell anyone you'll be home alone, even friends at school.

4 TRUE OR FALSE? In case you lose power, you should know where candles and matches are kept.

5 TRUE OR FALSE? You should always answer the phone in case it's your parents trying to get in touch with you.

6 TRUE OR FALSE: If you arrive at home and the door to the house is open, you can go in, because no one would be burglarizing a house in the middle of the day.

7 TRUE OR FALSE? If there is a fire in the house, you should call 911 right away.

8 TRUE OR FALSE? Even if the stranger knocking at the door already knows that you're home, you shouldn't let him in.

Answers:

1. FALSE: You should keep the volume low so that you can be alert to what is happening in the house and yard.

2. FALSE: All guns should be stored, unloaded, in a locked gun cabinet with the ammunition stored in a separate location.

3. TRUE: Friends might be careless with the information and tell someone who could be a danger to you.

4. FALSE: You should know where flashlights (with new batteries) are kept. Never burn candles without parental supervision.

5. FALSE: You can always let the call go to the answering machine and listen to the message. If it turns out to be your mom or dad calling from an unfamiliar number, you can pick up the phone and talk.

6. FALSE: Never go into the house if the door is open or if it looks like someone might have broken in.

7. FALSE: You should leave your house immediately and call 911 from a neighbor's house.

8. TRUE: You should immediately call a parent and tell him or her what's happening. If you are worried that the person will try to get into the house, you should call 911.

Your Private Space at Home

"I found an old poster from Woodstock that my mom had in her college room a million years ago. I hung it up in my room and my friends think it's really cool!"
—Mandi

Your room should reflect your own personality, style, and interests. You're not a little kid anymore, so the room that your parents designed for you eons ago might not work for you now. You can make easy, inexpensive changes that will make your special space trendy and unique!

• Come up with a theme for your room. A theme might be the ocean, the color pink, or music. Anything you like can be turned into a theme for your room.

• Paint your room in a color that makes a statement about you! (Paint is the cheapest way to transform a room.) If you don't want to paint the whole room, just cover one wall with your new color, or paint stripes or polka dots on a wall.

• If you're artistic, paint a mural! Or use stencils or large stamps to create your very own "wallpaper."

• Use adhesive (but removable!) decals to jazz up your walls. You can find polka dots, sports, animals, and many other decal themes.

• For a place to jot down notes (and for friends to leave messages), paint a section of wall with chalkboard paint.

• Push a twin bed against a wall and put pillows along the back so that it has the feel of a couch for when friends come over.

• Hang twinkly holiday lights for a permanently festive look. (You can even hang star or snowflake ornaments from the ceiling!)

• Exchange the old toy box for some cool baskets that can provide storage. For unseen storage, buy under-the-bed containers and tuck away things like off-season clothes and extra school supplies.

- Hang a corkboard and message board so that you can tack up school paperwork and leave yourself reminders about important dates and events.

- Think about creating a special nook for reading or listening to music using beaded curtains, a canopy, or a room divider.

- Show off a collection that is important to you. Do you have swimming ribbons or trophies? Stuffed penguins? Decorative boxes? To make the most of your collection, don't scatter the items around the room. Instead, cluster them together. Maybe your mom or dad can make a high shelf for your display.

- Fabric can be expensive, but often colorful, patterned sheets go on sale. You can make curtains or pillows from a sheet set for next to nothing!

- Update an old dresser by buying cool new knobs!

- Go "shopping" in your attic or basement. You may find some bookshelves you can paint, or some vintage suitcases that you can use for storage and stack on top of one another as a side table. Be creative!

- If you want a more drastic change, see if you can switch rooms with a sibling, or maybe fix up a part of the house (in the basement perhaps?) for a special teen space.

- If you don't sew, you can re-cover an old pillow by buying two pieces of fleece from a craft or department store. Cut the edges all around into a three-inch long fringe and then tie the top piece of fringe to the one below it to create a pillow cover!

Top Tip

After you choose a paint color, pick out two or three other colors that complement the main one and look for pillows, curtains, and other accessories with these colors on them.

Secrets of Sharing Space

Sharing a room with a sister can be problematic. Not only are there issues of privacy, but decorating, too: She might love pink and butterflies while you are all about blue and soccer. Here are a few tips:

• Choose a main color you both like, then accessorize your separate beds and areas with complementary colors of your own choosing. If the main color of the room is light blue, you might choose green as your second color and your sister might choose pink.

• If you have bunk buds, the girl with the top bunk can have her favorite color on the top half of the walls and the girl with the bottom bunk can choose the color for the lower half. (Of course, the colors need to complement each other for this to look good.)

• Have three zones in the room: a private zone for each of you as well as a shared zone.

• If you want to divide the room and create privacy, hang a curtain in the middle of the room (the way hospitals have curtains on tracks around beds) or place a long, low bookcase in the middle of the room.

• Set aside specific times of the day for each of you to be alone in the room.

• Try having a rule where you spend 10 minutes picking up before you go to bed. That way, one person's mess never gets completely out of control.

• Agree to (and write down) the rules of the room so there are fewer misunderstandings. Include rules for friends who visit, playing music, and lights out.

"I really wanted to put a lock on my door but my parents wouldn't let me. They did let me put up a sign that says "Please respect my privacy" on one side and "Come on in" on the other, so that I can let everyone know when I want some time alone. They make me have the 'come in' side facing out at least half of the time, though!"
—Leanna

"One of the worst punishments I ever got was when I slammed the door to my room one too many times and my dad came up and took the door off the hinges! For two weeks I had no door!"
—Savannah

Sibling Rivalry

Maybe you and your sister are best friends. Maybe you can't stand to be in the same room together. Maybe it depends on the day: Some days you love hanging out with her and some days you can't say a word to each other without arguing!

Sibling rivalry, which can include competition, jealousy, and anger among brothers and sisters, is very common. You are all competing for your parents' love and attention. You all have different personalities and different needs, and yet are living in the same space. The good news is that because you're stuck with each other, you *have* to work things out! You will learn how to handle conflict and come up with solutions to problems better than kids without siblings.

Even though it's natural to feel jealous over the attention your sibling gets from your parent, it's important not to overreact. Try to be objective when you

Fun FAcT

Things are better now than when you were little: Kids between 2 and 4 years old fight about every 9 minutes!

"Sometimes I just need to get away from my sister because she drives me nuts. My mom talked to my aunt and every few weeks I go over to her house. She lives alone and we do fun stuff together like paint our nails and go shopping. Most of all, it doesn't involve my little sister!"
— Kaylie

"I fight a lot with my little brother at home, but if anyone else ever said or did something to hurt him, I would totally protect him!"
— Maya

are tempted to accuse your parents of favoring your sister or brother. If your mom says to your sister, "Wow! Great job on the math test," don't replay that in your head as "Wow! You are a math genius and so much better in math than anyone else in the family!" That's not what your mom said. Think of it this way: Your mom makes yummy cookies. Do you think less of your dad because your mom is a great baker? Of course not! You think that he tells the funniest jokes ever! Telling your mom that her cookies are great is not a slam against your dad!

Sometimes, parents compliment their kids when they achieve something that has been difficult for them in the past. Maybe they are overly excited about your brother scoring a goal in soccer because he hasn't done that before. If you think of it that way, you can be happy for him, too, rather than feeling bummed or resentful.

What kinds of compliments do your parents give you? They probably praise you for lots of things you do! Take in those kind words and don't waste time comparing the number of times they complimented you versus the number of times they complimented your brother or sister. Not important! And rather than resenting the privileges your sibs have, think about what *you're* allowed to do. Do your parents let you go to the late movie with friends, go midnight bowling, or have sleepovers once a month?

The question to ask yourself is: Are my parents doing their best to be fair? Kids require different things at different times. It's not practical to treat every child exactly the same way. You and your siblings have very different needs. As long as your mom and dad seem to be trying to treat you all fairly, do your best to rise above any pettiness.

Fun FAcT

There's good news about having a brother or sister! A national study showed that children with siblings are more aware of other people's feelings, express their own feelings more positively, tend to make friends more easily, and are more likely to accept children who are different from them.

Things Your Parents Can Do to Help with Sibling Rivalry

Ask your parents to....

...avoid comparing you to your siblings.

...listen to you when you need to explain what is bothering you about your siblings.

...refrain from making you be the parent to a younger brother or sister.

...spend one-on-one time with you, as well as with your siblings.

...take you to a private place if they need to scold you, rather than do it in front of your siblings.

...make sure chores are assigned fairly.

...avoid labeling you or your siblings as the "smart one" or the "athletic one."

...make sure they never play favorites.

...support you when you try to have private time, and allow you to keep some belongings to yourself rather than having to share everything.

...try to solve their own relationship issues in a quiet, respectful way.

"I used to get really mad at the fact that my parents were always making a big deal about my little brother. But then I realized that he's not in school yet, and so they are the only ones who really say anything at all to him. I am lucky because my teachers, my swim coach, and my friends all say nice things about me all the time!"
—Josie

"My brother and I always used to fight about who got to ride 'shot gun' in the car. Finally my mom said that when the date is an even number, like June 2, I get to ride in the front and when it's an odd date, my brother gets to."
—Janelle

"I always like playing with my little brother because it gives me an excuse to play with toys that are really too young for me. He likes to play with Legos and Playmobil, and so do I."
—Toni

Idea!

Find activities that require you and your sibling to cooperate and be a good team. Can you play a musical duet together? Can you team up in Pictionary against your parents?

Sibling Strain

No one knows how to push your buttons like your brother or sister! If you have a sibling who's driving you crazy, and you've tried everything you can to work it out on your own, see if you can get your parents' help in establishing some ground rules like these:

- Knock before entering my room.
- Ask before borrowing anything of mine.
- Never read my texts, emails, or any other personal correspondence.
- If I have friends over, please respect my privacy.
- If you have friends over, please don't treat me badly to show off for your friends.
- Never hurt me physically or say cruel things that are meant to hurt me.

107

Parent Problems

You and your mom used to be buds. You always thought of yourself as Daddy's little girl. Suddenly, things aren't going as well as they used to. You and your mom can't seem to agree on anything, and your dad seems confused and detached. What's up?

Your world is getting bigger and you are getting more independent (but you still rely on your parents for *a lot)*. As you negotiate aspects of your newfound freedom with your mom and dad, you're bound to clash. You want to see PG-13 movies, or wear makeup, or date, and your parents don't think you're ready for those things. The issue is not who's right and who's wrong, but how to talk about things in a productive way.

There's usually a compromise that can be reached so that you and your parents are satisfied. Maybe you can't wear eyeliner and mascara, but your mom gives you the thumbs up on blush and lip-gloss. Your parents might not want you to go to the theater to see a PG-13 movie, but they'll agree to let you rent one to watch at home, so they can check it out, too. And maybe you won't be able to go on a bona-fide date, but your folks might allow a group date, where you'll have other kids with you.

Sometimes the difference between hearing a YES from your parents and hearing a NO comes down to timing and delivery. What does that mean? It means that you need to choose a good time to talk to your folks and deliver the message in a way that will make them hear you and want to work with you.

"I had a hard time convincing my mom to let me get instant messaging. I felt so out of the loop without it."
—Shelby

Fun FAcT

Four out of five teenagers have cell phones and about half of kids between the ages of 8 and 12 have their own phones. The average child gets her first cell phone when she is 10 or 11 years old.

Seven Secrets for Getting Your Parents to Listen to Your Side of the Story

1 Plan ahead. Ask your mom or dad, "When is a good time to talk?"

2 Talk somewhere quiet and private, where siblings won't interrupt. If there's no quiet spot in the house, maybe you can take a walk or go for a car ride.

3 Plan what you will say before you start, trying to think from the point of view of a parent. Be specific in what you want or need. ("I'd like to go to the Rec Center dance this Friday night.")

4 Patiently wait for an answer. The harder you push, the more they'll push back.

5 If you don't get the answer you want, ask respectfully for an explanation. ("Can you tell me why you're worried about the dance?")

6 Offer suggestions as to how you could compromise. ("What if you pick me up an hour early from the dance?" "What if I find out if any of the chaperones are adults you know?")

7 If you still don't hear the answer you want, don't get angry. Act mature. Ask, "Is there anything I can do to earn your trust so that you might say yes in the future?" That'll really impressive 'em!

"I'm a Mormon so my parents are pretty strict. They weren't crazy about the idea of me going to the middle school dances. Instead I went to the Mormon dances that my church organized. I always had so much fun and met really cool people! In eighth grade, I went to the last school dance of the year, and in comparison, the Mormon dances I went to were so much more fun... Instead of grinding and making out, girls and boys actually *danced* with each other and *talked* to each other. I don't regret skipping school dances at all!"
—Mary Ann

Fun FAcT

Four thousand girls answered an online poll that asked: What do your parents bug you about the most? Just over half said that they got hassled about keeping their rooms clean, a quarter said that they are nagged about finishing homework, and 8 percent said that their parents complain about their cell phone bills. A whopping 17 percent reported that their parents don't bother them about anything! Wow!

"I know my mom and I will be best friends when I'm older, but it's hard right now because she just doesn't understand my life."
—Caroline

"If my parents are in a lecturing, ranting, yelling mood, I give them time to calm down and then I go back later and ask them for a ride, money, or whatever, once they've cooled down and are being more rational."
—Meg

Here's What Girls Had to Say When Asked What Made Them Happiest About Their Moms:

"My mom will always listen to my problems, even if they are the same problems everyday."

"She's really happy for me when things go well."

"She loves me no matter what."

"My mom would always help me out if I asked her to."

"She gives me really good advice when I ask for it."

"My mom knows me better than anyone else in the world."

"My mom can always make me laugh when I've had a rotten day."

Here's What Girls Had to Say When Asked What Bothered Them the Most About Their Moms:

"My mom won't listen to a logical argument."

"My mom doesn't care about my opinion at all."

"She needs to know every single detail of my life."

"My mom always bugs me about cleaning my room and doing my homework."

"She tries to tell me what to eat."

"She has no idea what it's like to be a kid today; her advice is from, like, the '50s."

"She says things that embarrass me in front of my friends."

Sometimes the problem with parents is about more than a tug-of-war over how much freedom you should have. There may be other issues. Maybe your parents push you too hard, expecting straight As or pressuring you to be involved in too many extracurricular activities. They probably think they're being supportive, but they are making you feel too stressed. In a survey sponsored in part by the Girl Scouts, kids ages 8 to 12 reported feeling a lot of pressure to make their parents proud and do well in school. Seventy-one percent said they worry about having harder homework, 59 percent were nervous about getting good grades, and 43 percent were concerned with making their parents proud of them.

Speaking to your parents in a logical, calm way will help you make your case if you feel you have too much pressure in your life. Come to them with a solution as well as a problem: "If I don't do the school play this year, that will leave me more time to work on math, because I'm struggling in that class."

If you feel that they are still not receptive, you might need to speak to a guidance counselor at school, and she can help you deliver the message to your folks that you are having a hard time coping with all of the stress in your life.

7 Important Things to Tell Your Parents if They Get Divorced

You may need to remind your parents what your needs are during and after their divorce. If it's hard for you to talk to them, then write a letter to them both expressing how you feel. Here are some things you might want to say:

1 I need both of you in my life.

2 Please don't argue in front of me, especially when it's *about* me. Work things out when I'm not around.

3 Please don't ask me a million questions about the other household or the other parent. It makes me feel disloyal to him or her.

4 Please don't use me to deliver money or messages.

5 Never use me to hurt the other parent by saying that he or she can't see me because you're angry.

6 Please don't "trash talk" the other parent. Instead of convincing me to be on your side, it makes me want to defend the one you are bashing.

7 Please don't act sad and jealous if I want to spend time with the other parent. It doesn't mean that I don't love you. But it does make me feel guilty and unhappy when you do that.

A lot of middle school girls complain that their parents embarrass them. Maybe they share things about you with their friends that you wish they wouldn't. Maybe your mom insists on walking with you into a new friend's house so that she can meet everyone. If you tell your parents that they embarrass you, they will probably tell you stories about how *their* parents embarrassed *them!* It's a common problem pre-teens and teens have faced for a long time! No matter what the issue, the best strategy is to talk to them about your concerns in a calm way when no one is upset.

The Girls Scouts survey also showed that the relationship that tweens have with the adults in their lives is a huge source of confidence for them. Nine out of every ten tweens reported that the way they are treated by parents and other relatives, as well as by teachers, makes them feel good about themselves. So even if all is not perfect at home, it's worth putting a lot of effort into keeping the relationship with your parents solid.

Middle School Girls in Action!

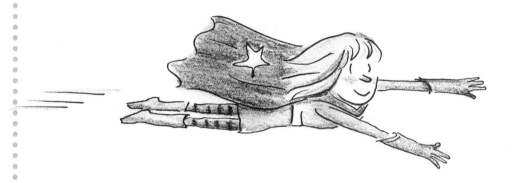

Cell Phones for Soldiers

Five years ago, 13-year old Brittany Bergquist and her younger brother heard of a soldier who owed thousands of dollars because of cell phone calls to his family while serving overseas. Shocked and upset, Brittany decided that they had to help find a way for soldiers to talk to their families for free. So the siblings collected old cell phones and other electronics that could be recycled for money in the same way you can recycle soda cans. Brittany and her brother used the money they earned to buy pre-paid phone cards for soldiers. Today, with cell-phone collection boxes in all 50 states and Canada, Brittany's nonprofit organization has raised millions of dollars, enabling 450,000 pre-paid phone cards to be purchased for soldiers who want to call their families!

Cinderella's Closet

When Student Council vice-president Sarah Turnbull* sat in the school lunchroom selling tickets for the holiday dance, she was saddened by how many girls told her that they couldn't afford the $5 ticket price. She realized that if they didn't have enough money for the ticket, they certainly didn't have enough money to buy a fancy dress. She thought about how lucky she was to get hand-me-downs from her older sister Samantha, which gave her a great idea. That night, she asked Samantha if she would collect dresses that her high school friends had outgrown to donate to middle school girls. Sam agreed. Then Sarah spoke to her school principal, who assigned one of the guidance counselors to turn a closet in her office into a space to store the dresses. Sarah collected 30 dresses for that year's holiday dance, and "Cinderella's Closet" continues today, even though Sarah is now in college!

*Name changed

Animals in Action

When she was just 9 years old, Scottsdale, Arizona's Sara Carrington came up with a creative way to raise money to buy supplies for homeless animals that she named "Animals in Action." She began sketching pictures of people's pets and accepting donations for each drawing. The donations paid for collars, leashes, toys, and other items for cats and dogs at the Animal Rescue Center, a no-kill shelter in Phoenix.

Bracelets for Cancer Research

Twelve-year old Abby Lowther from South Carolina raised $500 for cancer research by making bracelets. She began making the bracelets to raise money for Relay for Life because a classmate, Bradley Stanley was battling cancer and she wanted to help. Inside every bracelet she put three pink stones representing faith, hope, and love. She felt that her gesture showed that if everyone did something to help, no matter how small, it would make a big difference.

Helping with Horses

One Virginia 12-year old turned her love of horses into a gift for disabled children. Julie Kroll volunteers with Wonderkids, a project that helps handicapped children through equestrian therapy. The participating children have disabilities ranging from Down's syndrome to cerebral palsy to attention deficit disorder (ADD). Julie uses her knowledge of horses and riding to adapt the session to each particular child. The program director feels that Julie has a special bond with the children and has a calming effect on them. For the past three years, Julie has volunteered every week for three to four hours a day.

What Can You Do to Help?

You don't have to make a huge gesture…you can start small! Go through your closet and fill a bag with clothes that don't fit or that are no longer your style. Donate the clothes to a local Salvation Army or Goodwill so that someone less fortunate can wear them! Or start a No Trash Tuesday or No Waste Wednesday at school, where everyone tries to use recyclable items rather than throwing disposable ones away. What great ideas do you and your friends have for helping others?

Chapter 6

Body Secrets

> "In my group of friends, I'm the only one who doesn't wear a bra and hasn't gotten her period. I don't want to be left out of all of the conversations, so I constantly ask people for advice about things, like they're the smart, knowing ones. Everyone loves to give advice to other people, right? They practically fight over who gets to tell me how to hide tampons on your way to the bathroom and stuff like that!"
> —Bridget

Middle school is a time when you'll have all sorts of questions about your body, from how to buy a bra to how to apply eyeliner! There's a lot to learn as your body and your priorities start to change. In fact, there's so much information that this chapter could easily be a book in itself! Because not every topic can be covered in detail, you'll read about where you can go for more information on specific issues.

For girls, puberty begins between the ages of 8 and 13. This means that certain hormones will cause changes in your size and shape as your body becomes a woman's body. Every girl develops at her own pace, so try hard not to compare yourself to your friends. Some girls are done developing by seventh grade, while others haven't even started at that point! Rather than focusing on what you want to change about your own body or rate of growth, pay attention to what you like. Do you have long, shiny hair or beautiful brown eyes? Long legs that run fast or strong arms that help you smack a tennis ball? What do you love the most about yourself?

Helpful Body Books

The Care and Keeping of You: The Body Book for Girls is a bestselling book from American Girl that answers all sorts of questions you might have about your body and how it's changing. (The same folks also put out a great book called *Is This Normal?*)

It's a Girl Thing by Mavis Jukes is a bit more advanced. If you have questions that aren't addressed in this chapter (such as questions about sex or birth control) you might want to read this honest guide.

The Girl's Body Book is written by a nurse, Kelli Dunham, who offers advice on everything from your first visit to the gynecologist to coping with divorce.

Body Size and Body Image

Some girls have larger frames and some have smaller ones. It all depends on your genes as well as how you eat and exercise. Even though puberty normally ends at 17, some girls will have reached their adult height by the end of middle school! Others will have just started to grow at that point. There is never a greater variety of body shapes and sizes than there is in middle school!

You may want to change certain things about your body, like your weight, but you should ask your doctor about that first. He may tell you that you are the perfect size for your body type or he may tell you that your body is changing and you need to be patient! One thing that happens to girls during puberty is that weight is distributed differently around the body. Your waist, for instance, may become a bit thicker. But that is just for now. Some girls suddenly gain weight; then several months later, their height catches up!

If she thinks it's right for you, your doctor may help you make some dietary and fitness changes that will help you achieve a healthier body. The important thing is to accept and embrace the parts of you that can't be changed and

Top Tip

Don't compare yourself to models or celebrities in magazines! Many of those photos are altered to make the women look super skinny with no flaws! One famous model, Cindy Crawford, once said, "Even *I* don't look like Cindy Crawford!" meaning that in real life, she doesn't look anything like her magazine photos!

Fun FAcT

In a poll of preteens, 82 percent of the girls reported liking themselves "a lot!"

Sleepy Secrets

Guess how many hours of sleep are recommended for girls your age? Nine! If you get regular exercise, avoid drinking anything with caffeine after dinner, and develop a nighttime routine (for instance, take a bath, then read a chapter of your favorite book) you should have no trouble falling asleep *and* staying asleep! (If yours is a noisy nighttime house, you may want to run a fan in your room to drown out the sounds.)

come up with a sensible plan to change things that will keep your body healthy and strong.

It's important to remember that every girl who looks around her school will be able to find someone she thinks has nicer hair, or looks better in jeans or in sweaters. And while you are looking at other girls, they are looking at you, wishing they had your eyes, or your smile, or your beautiful skin! Nearly every girl is overly aware of the things she would like to change about herself and not nearly happy enough about her wonderful assets! Play a game with your best friends where you take turns paying each other compliments. You will be surprised at all of the great things your friends have noticed about you!

> "I went to a private school and had a really small class. I was the *only* tall girl. We did this thing in science where we had to put our height and weight on the board. Everyone knew which measurements were mine because they were so much bigger than everyone else's. I had to convince everyone in my class that I weighed 20 pounds more than they did because I was 6 inches taller than them!"
> —Shelly

> "Now I look back at middle school and I'm like 'I was tiny!' but at the time, this mean girl would call me a 'fat pig' and I let it go to my head. I can't believe I let myself be bothered by people who were just trying to hurt my feelings for no reason."
> —Ellie

Fun FAcTs

Seal, the musician who is married to supermodel Heidi Klum, says that "true beauty is internal and eternal."

Supermodel Cindy Crawford has said, "I often tell young women that my shortcoming became ironically my trademark and I encourage them to love everything about themselves—even the parts which are not perfect."

Supermodel Tyra Banks was very skinny and gangly when she was a pre-teen. She has unhappy memories of being teased about her unattractive looks.

Fun FAcT

Sixty percent of girls say they are trying to lose weight; only 16 percent of girls ages 6 to 19 are actually overweight.

Celebrities Who Celebrate Their Flaws—and Their Individuality!

These celebs certainly have the means to change whatever they want to about themselves, but they choose not to! They like the features that make them special! Here is a list of a few well-known stars and what some would call their "flaws":

Madonna, musician, and Anna Paquin, actor: Gap between the front teeth

Tyra Banks, supermodel: Large forehead (she calls it her "five-head")

Cindy Crawford, supermodel: Mole above her lip

Jewel, musician, and Kirsten Dunst, actor: Crooked tooth

Barack Obama, politician: Prominent ears

Tina Fey, actor: Facial scars from a childhood attack by a stranger

Sarah Jessica Parker, actor: Distinctive nose

Seal, musician: Facial scars from a childhood disease

Karolina Kurkova, supermodel: No belly button because of a childhood operation

Kate Hudson, actor: Eyes set far apart (she was called "Hammerhead" as a child, like the shark)

Milo Ventimiglia, actor: A crooked smile due to a birth defect

Fueling a Healthy Body

In order to operate at its peak, your body needs the right kinds of food in the right amounts. The most important thing to remember is that you want to eat a balanced diet. A balanced diet can include fun foods like fries and ice cream, but not all the time and not in huge amounts.

It's important to eat three meals a day, in addition to healthy snacks. Some girls skip breakfast, but this is not a good idea. Studies have shown that kids who eat breakfast have better memories and test scores, longer attention spans, and healthier body weighs than kids who skip breakfast. If you don't like traditional breakfast food, get creative! Mix fresh fruit into yogurt, roll scrambled eggs into a warm tortilla, or eat a slice of cold pizza! If you are running late in the morning, grab an apple, a muffin, or a hard-boiled egg to eat on the way to the bus stop.

Some middle school girls experiment with specialized diets, like vegan or vegetarian diets. It is very hard (but not impossible) to get the nutrients your growing body needs if you eliminate certain food groups altogether. Your doctor can help you come up with a nutrition plan that will work for you.

> "The girls who bragged about skipping breakfast and who never ate anything at lunch were the girls who actually tended to be heavier. It's like they were so starving when they got home that they just ate everything in sight!"
> —Caitlin

If you and your doctor agree that you can safely follow an alternative diet, you may need to carry some snacks with you for times when you don't have access to the kinds of foods you want. If your friends act like they think what you're doing is weird, invite them over and cook a vegetarian or vegan meal together! Show them how tasty and creative other recipes can be!

You should definitely pay attention to your iron intake, especially after you start getting your period. Iron is important because it helps your blood cells carry oxygen, and that affects your energy level. If you don't have enough healthy red blood cells, you may become anemic. This will make you feel weak and tired. Middle school girls need about 8 milligrams of iron every day to avoid becoming anemic. Red meat, eggs, fish, and fortified cereals are great ways to get iron. A cup of Cheerios has more than 10 milligrams and whole grain Total has over 22!

Secrets for Eating Healthier

It's easy to eat healthy if you follow a few simple rules:

- Eat when you are truly hungry, not out of boredom or habit.

- Don't skip lunch as a way to diet. You'll feel tired and listless all afternoon (and you'll be so hungry when you get home from school that you'll take in more calories than if you'd had just eaten a regular lunch).

- Drink a glass of water if you've recently had a healthy meal or snack but you still feel hungry. Sometimes our bodies fool us into thinking we're hungry when actually we're thirsty.

- Eat at the kitchen table, not in front of the TV. When you are distracted while eating, you tend to eat more than you realize without really tasting the food!

- Make good choices for afternoon snacks like carrots, celery sticks, cherry tomatoes, apples, bananas, grapes, raisins, dried fruit, yogurt, nuts, popcorn, pretzels, or string cheese.

- Substitute water (or vitamin water) for soda.

- Sneak healthy foods into things you already like. Ask your mom or dad to help you add shredded carrots to a muffin mix or spinach to spaghetti sauce.

- Ask your parents to buy snacks in single serving sizes or divide a large bag of chips into smaller baggies so that you're aware of exactly how big a snack you're having.

Check Out These Websites for More Info:

www.mypyramid.gov to find out what makes a balanced diet for a girl your age

http://www.beaconstreetgirls.com/avery/healthy-eating-in-the-caf to learn how to eat healthy in the school cafeteria

http://www.kewlbites.com to see what Reed Alexander, who plays the evil Nevel on the hit TV show iCarly, advises for kids who want to eat better

"My mom makes me breakfast, lunch, and dinner every day that I'm home. In our house, meals are about family, not counting carbs."
—Mary Ann

Is Fast Food Bad?

No food is a "bad" food. Fast food is, however, made with cheap ingredients and is often high in fat and calories, so you can't eat it all the time if you want to stay healthy. For the times when you do eat fast food, make healthier choices, ordering the grilled items (rather than the fried ones), and using mustard or ketchup instead of mayo. Also, order regular or kid-size portions (no super sizing!), add lettuce and tomato to a burger or sandwich, and choose low-fat milk or fruit juice rather than soda. For the other two meals of the day, make sure to load up on fruit and veggies!

Fun FAcT

According to one expert, it takes an average of 66 days to cement a new habit like eating fruit with lunch or running every day after school. That may seem like a long time, but once you establish a habit, it doesn't take a lot of effort to keep it going.

Eating Disorders

Some girls can develop eating disorders, becoming so obsessed with losing weight that they change their eating habits entirely. Anorexia nervosa causes girls to try to avoid eating altogether so that they begin to starve themselves. Bulimia is a disorder that makes girls want to overeat, and then vomit or use laxatives to get the food out of their bodies. Both of these can have horrible consequences if they are untreated. These problems are too serious for girls to handle alone. Ask a trusted adult for help if you or a friend has an eating disorder.

Top Tip

Middle school girls recommend the novel *Perfect* by Natasha Friend, which follows 13-year old Isabelle Lee through her battle with an eating disorder. You can also check out the National Eating Disorders Association for information: http://www.nationaleatingdisorders.org/information-resources/

"Do a sport so that you focus more on what your body can *do* rather than what it looks like. Plus, your body just *feels* better when you're exercising!"

—Kendall

Move it!

Exercise is important because it boosts your energy level and helps you maintain a weight that is right for you. Pediatricians recommend that you exercise enough to raise your heart rate and make you breathe hard. It's important to gently stretch your muscles before and after a workout, and to drink plenty of water.

Exercise should be fun, and easy to work into your daily life. Sometimes you can make small changes to your daily routine that increase the amount of exercise you get, like walking to school rather than taking the bus. Here are great ideas from middle school girls who have found enjoyable ways to get exercise!

"My friends and I love to go to the playground and run around! We feel like little kids again!"

"I take two dance classes: ballet and jazz. It's so much fun I don't even think about the fact that it's exercise."

"I walk my dog twice a day."

"My neighbor and I ride our bikes to school and back every day."

"I love to play flashlight tag with the other kids in the neighborhood!"

"My best friend and I walk to the YMCA after school and then go on the climbing wall."

"A bunch of kids stay after school and we play ultimate Frisbee on the fields in back."

All About Breasts and Bras

Sometime after age 9, you'll notice that your breasts begin to change. Breast buds develop first, then the nipple and the area around it (the areola) grow and darken in color. As the breasts get a little larger, they may start out looking "pointy" but will soon fill in and become rounder. As some girls develop, they find the nipple and areola grow as a mound before the areola eventually flattens out and blends into the breast, with the nipple coming out of the areola in the shape of a pencil eraser. About 3 to 5 years after your breasts start growing, they will reach their full size. Your genes determine what your breasts will eventually look like. (Exercise, creams, and other products will not affect breast size.)

Top Tip

For detailed health information aimed at teen girls, check out **www.youngwomenshealth.org.**

What About...

... one breast that seems to be growing faster than the other?
Not to worry. They will most likely be close in size when they are fully developed (but no one has two identical breasts). Specialty bra shops sell foam inserts that you can slip into your bra if you are self-conscious about the size difference.

...inverted nipples?
Normal, and not a problem. In a group of ten girls, one or two have inverted nipples. Be sure to wash them well so that you don't develop an infection in the skin creases.

...hair that grows around the nipple?
Again, normal. Don't try to pull the hairs out; that might cause an infection. You can trim the hair with small fingernail scissors, or just let it be!

...breasts that are kind of pointy?
Often, breasts look a bit pointy in the earlier stages of development. They will eventually have a rounder shape.

... breasts that seem to hang low?
Whether they point upward, hang down, are big and round, or small and dainty, they are all perfectly normal breasts.

...breasts that are sore?
You may experience some soreness in your breasts as they develop or just before you get your period each month. This is normal, and you can take medication like ibuprofen if you are uncomfortable.

You'll want to buy a bra when you think that wearing one would make you feel more comfortable. This might be when you are self-conscious about your breasts showing through your shirt or bouncing when you move around in gym class. Ask your mom, aunt, or grandmother to take you shopping.

When people refer to bra sizes, they mention a number and a letter. The number has to do with the measurement around your rib cage, just under your breasts. If the measurement is 24 inches, for instance, you would add 5 or 6 inches to arrive at your number, which would be 30. (It's always an even number.)

Fun FAcT

Lady Gaga has said about her middle school and high school years, "I used to get made fun of for being either too provocative or too eccentric, so I started to tone it down. I didn't fit in, and I felt like a freak."

"Before I got my first bra, I just wore tank tops under my shirts. My friend Elena wore sports bras first because they looked like short tanks."

—Gianna

"My breasts got really big, really fast. I was completely developed by the end of middle school. I got a lot of attention from boys but it felt creepy, not good."

—Amanda

Top Tip

You don't need to wear a bra at night. You'll be more comfortable without one.

The letter refers to the cup size of the bra, which has to do with the size of your breasts. The way to determine your cup size is to have your mom or aunt measure around your bust line, or the fullest part of your breasts. From this number, subtract the number you got when you measured around your rib cage and added 5 or 6. If the difference between the two numbers is ½, you are an AA cup; if it's 1, you are an A cup, 2 you are a B cup, and so on. You will likely begin with an AA or A size and the bra might be called a "training bra."

You will need to try on a variety of bras because you'll notice that one 32A bra might fit perfectly while two more might not fit at all. Different styles fit very differently. You can also adjust the shoulder strap length and you'll have a few choices as you hook the bra in back, making it tighter or looser.

Secrets for Shaving Your Legs and Underarms

You may notice underarm hair beginning to grow and want to shave it. Or you may want to shave the hair on your legs. (Most girls just shave the hair below the knee, which can be more noticeable than the finer hair above the knee.) Often girls in middle school will begin to shave these two areas, and shaving is an easy thing to learn to do. But the choice of whether or not to shave is up to you.

Shave when you are in the shower or bathtub so that your skin is wet. Use shaving cream made for teen skin (or soap, in a pinch). Move the razor up your leg or down your armpit, rinsing the razor often so that the hair doesn't build up. It can be a bit tricky to figure out how hard to press on the razor. Start off gently, and press harder as you need to. Make sure you don't use a dull blade, which can irritate your skin. After you shave your legs and pat them dry, you can put some lotion on them.

Sexual Harassment

is when someone makes rude gestures or comments about your body, or touches or rubs up against you. Sexual harassment is against the law when it happens at school, and you should report it to a teacher or other adult right away.

Your Period

You will probably start your period after age 9 and before age 15, with the average being around 12 years old. Your period may start a year or two after your breasts begin to develop, you notice underarm and pubic hair, and you sometimes find light colored fluid in your underpants. The idea of getting your period can be a little scary, but learning as much as you can will help prepare you.

Many girls worry about when they might get their first period. It's true that you won't know when your period is coming, but you can be prepared for that time so that there is no drama and panic involved! You will know you have your period when you see a red or brownish stain in your underpants. Keep pads in your backpack and in your locker, just in case. (Folding toilet paper and putting it in your underpants like a pad will do if you're stuck.) Also keep an extra pair of underpants and jeans in your locker (or your gym locker) if there's room. Many girls suggest having a sweatshirt available to tie around your waist if you get your period when you aren't expecting it.

You can always go to the school nurse or your guidance counselor if you need help during the school day. Not only has every adult woman been through this, but people who work in middle schools help out with this issue all the time.

Even though the flow during your period usually lasts from three to seven days, your first period will often be brief. It may take a few months, or even years, for your body to settle into a regular pattern. When it does, your period will likely come every month or so. On average, you will lose about 4 to 6 tablespoons of fluid during the time you have your period. You will be able to tell when your period is coming to an end each month because you'll recognize the pattern: a heavy flow in the middle and a light one at the end, with the color often becoming darker. You'll want to mark the days you have your period on a calendar so that you can try to anticipate when it will come. (Wear dark colored pants as you get close to the time you expect your period to start.)

If you get cramps, you can take Tylenol or a special medicine made for menstrual cramps. Ask your mom or another adult woman what would be best.

What Exactly Is Your Period?

Your menstruation period is the time each month or so when fluid containing blood flows out of your uterus and through your vagina. This fluid builds up on the walls of your uterus every month. If you become pregnant someday, the lining will serve as a kind of nest for the growing baby. In the meantime, the lining sheds itself every month or so, which is your period!

Pads versus Tampons

Pads usually have a strip on the back that you can peel off so that they will stick to your underpants. There are maxi pads for your heaviest days and panty liners for days when you think you might be getting your period or for when your period is just about over and the flow is very light. You might also want to wear a panty liner with a tampon for extra protection. You'll want to change pads every few hours, even if it could absorb a bit more, just to prevent odors.

Tampons are cotton plugs that you insert into your vagina using an applicator so that the fluid is absorbed inside your body. The muscles in your vagina hold the tampon in place and a string hangs down so that you can pull the tampon out to change it. Girls who are very active may want to try tampons because it will make doing sports a little easier. Tampon sizes vary from junior to super plus or ultra.

Fun FAcT

Almost 4,000 pre-teen and teen girls responded to a survey about what they use when they have their periods. Fifty-five percent use pads, 19 percent use tampons, and 26 percent haven't gotten their periods yet.

Information is power! The more you know about your period, the better prepared you will be to handle it!

What if...

...you have a "leak" away from home?

You can tuck paper towels, napkins, or toilet paper into your underpants in a pinch. Borrow a jacket or sweatshirt to tie around your waist if you think something has leaked through your pants. Next time, wear both a tampon and a pad for extra protection.

...you are away from home and need to dispose of a pad or tampon?

NEVER flush a pad down the toilet (and to be safe, you probably shouldn't flush a tampon or applicator either). Use toilet paper to wrap around the pad and toss it into the nearest trashcan. In a public restroom, you'll often be able to put it in a small metal bin especially for used pads. In the worst-case scenario, you may have to tuck your wrapped bundle into your purse and look for a discreet place to throw it out.

...your flow is so heavy on some days that one pad isn't enough at night?

You can double up on pads, although what makes it tricky is that you move around at night and sleep in lots of different positions. If you've tried everything else, you can ask your mom or another adult woman who is close to you to buy adult diapers, which are just disposable underpants that absorb any leaks. No one needs to know you use these now and then! If you put one on with your pad, then any flow is contained in the underpants, which you throw out in the morning.

... you just put in a tampon and now you have to go to the bathroom?

Try holding the tampon string up and out of the way while you go. It is probably easier to coordinate tampon changing with your regular visit to use the bathroom if you can.

...you feel cramps in your abdomen before and during your period?

There are lots of different ways to relieve cramps: exercise, a hot bath, a hot-water bottle, and special medication that you can buy in the drug store. Ibuprofen works well, too! If your cramps are so severe that they regularly keep you home from school, you may need to ask your doctor what she suggests.

What Is PMS?

PMS is short for premenstrual syndrome. The hormonal changes that come with your period can make you feel different, physically and emotionally. You might notice cramps in your abdomen, a backache, sore breasts, overall puffiness, and maybe some pimples. You might also feel grumpier than usual. As soon as your period starts, your PMS will fade. Eat right, exercise, get enough sleep, and take pain medication if you need it.

Tampon Tips

Inserting a tampon can be a little tricky the first time, but it won't take long to get the hang of it. The best time to practice using a tampon is when your flow is the heaviest: the tampon will slide in more comfortably. (Before you start, take one or two tampons and practice pushing the tampon through the applicator so that you know how it works.)

First of all, relax your muscles so that the tampon will slide in more easily. Then sit on the toilet or stand with one foot on the closed toilet seat. Use one hand to hold the tampon applicator and the other to find the opening of your vagina. As you place the part of the applicator that holds the tampon into your vagina, use your index finger to gently press on the top part of the applicator until it is completely inside the bottom part of the applicator tube. This will push the

avoid getting an infection called toxic shock syndrome. (Use a maxi pad at night.)

Just relax and pull gently on the string to remove the used tampon.

tampon out of the applicator and into your vagina. (Don't worry—there's no way you can push it in too far.) You can slip the applicator out and throw it away. A string will hang down from the tampon; this is how you pull it out to change it. If it feels uncomfortable, you probably didn't push it in far enough. Gently pull it out and try again with a new tampon. (You can always put a little K-Y Jelly, which you can buy at any drug store, on the tip of the applicator so that it will slip in comfortably.) If you have trouble the first few times, don't worry. Set a goal for yourself of sliding the tampon in just a little bit further each time you try. The books previously recommended as well as some websites have more complete descriptions as well as illustrations showing how a tampon is inserted. Check out http://www.youngwomenshealth.org/tampon.html for helpful information and detailed diagrams.

You'll want to change a tampon every few hours, both to prevent leaks and to

Yikes! A Pimple!

No one escapes middle school without having a pimple, so while you may be suffering today, tomorrow it might be the cute guy in your math class!

Acne (another word for pimples and zits) is common for middle schoolers because the extra oil your body produces during puberty can clog your pores. If you have older brothers and sisters who suffered from acne, you might be more prone to pimples. There are a number of products you can find at the drug store to treat acne. An acne cream with salicylic acid or 2.5% benzoyl peroxide dabbed on pimples after you've washed your face may help dry them up. If your acne is more serious, your dermatologist (skin doctor) can prescribe a special lotion or even pills for you to take.

To help prevent pimples, wash your face gently each night with warm water and a cleanser meant especially for teenage faces. Make sure you wash away any makeup you put on during the day. (Waterproof mascara will require a special remover.) After you pat your face dry, you can put on facial lotion that is formulated for young skin. Look for the words "hypoallergenic" and "non-comedogenic" to identify products that are less likely to irritate your skin.

TOP Tip

You can also try dabbing the pimple with an ice cube to reduce swelling and redness.

To disguise the occasional pimple, there are a few simple secrets you should know. First, head for a drugstore (or a department store like Target or Wal-mart) and buy concealer in a color that matches your skin. It might look like a flesh-colored lipstick or a small tube of liquid in skin tone. Find a light powder that matches the color of the concealer. When you get home, wash and dry your face well. With a clean fingertip, apply just a dot of the concealer to the pimple. When the

TOP Tip

Zit rule number one: Don't squeeze it! It will look worse and be harder to disguise if you squeeze it. And if it gets infected, then you've got a real mess on your hands.

concealer is set, pat just a little powder on and around it. Now, leave it alone! (And pity the poor guys: They don't have the makeup options girls do to cover up those occasional zits!)

Idea!

There are lots of home remedies you can try to zap zits! For example, after washing your face, try putting a little dab of toothpaste on a pimple before you go to bed. It will dry out the pimple as you sleep! In the morning, gently wipe the toothpaste away with warm water and a soft washcloth. (Don't scrub it off!)

Secrets
for Coping With...

... freckles: You inherited your freckles. The only way to minimize them is to reduce your exposure to the sun: Wear lots of sunscreen and a baseball hat when you go outside—even in cloudy weather. (Self-tanners will make your skin darker, but will also darken your freckles.) Or, just embrace your unique look!

...stretch marks: Stretch marks (red lines on your skin) develop during adolescence when you experience a growth spurt. You may see them on your hips, thighs, or breasts. They will fade after a year or two, but there is nothing you can do in the meantime (so don't be tempted by those advertisements promising to get rid of them!).

... warts: A wart is caused by a virus; warts are very common for kids your age. Your local drugstore will have products that can help get rid of warts, and many of them look like ordinary band-aids. Your doctor can also help if those products don't work quickly or well enough.

... body odor: Shower every day and after exercising. Then use an antiperspirant/deodorant under your arms to help eliminate sweating and body odor. You'll have to decide whether you like solids, gels, or roll-ons. You might also try using nice smelling body washes in the shower.

... bad breath: Because bad breath is almost always caused by bacteria in the mouth, drinking plenty of water will help eliminate the problem. Brush and floss regularly, of course (and don't forget to brush your tongue!). Sugar-free gum will help if you're not able to get to your toothbrush.

... nail biting: Buy a special kind of polish to put on your nails that has a bitter taste and wear gloves to bed at night if you tend to bite your nails as you fall asleep. Some nail biters suggest chewing gum so that you are not tempted to chew on your nails!

... foot odor: Wear clean socks and shoes that are made of leather or canvas. You can buy special foot powders at the drug store or sprinkle some baking soda in your shoes when you take them off, leave it in there overnight, and dump it out in the morning.

...dark facial hair: You have several options if you are self-conscious about dark hair on your upper lip. You can buy a special product at the drugstore to bleach the hair so that it becomes very light, you can trim the hair frequently with blunt nail scissors, or you can have your upper lip waxed at a hair salon. When you are older, you can look into laser or electrolysis treatments.

...birth marks: You can find makeup that will cover many birthmarks, or you can talk to a dermatologist (skin doctor) about medical options for removing a birth mark. (Or you can learn to love your birthmark as something that makes you unique!)

Top Tip

If you wear a retainer, take it out in the bathroom and tuck it into its container before going to the cafeteria for lunch.

Braces

So many middle school kids have braces that sometimes it seems like the ones who *don't* have them are the odd ones! Braces can be a bit uncomfortable when they first go on, and then each time they are tightened, but the result is worth the inconvenience. When your braces come off, your teeth will be straight and you will smile with confidence!

You'll want to avoid foods that are sticky and high in sugar and take the time required to brush very, very well. If you don't, your teeth will have stains when the braces come off that are very hard and expensive to remove. Follow your orthodontist's instructions to the letter to be sure that the money and effort that are going into your braces will result in a perfect smile!

And as for that urban legend about braces getting locked together if two people kiss, not to worry. There is no evidence that anyone ever got her braces caught on someone else's during a kiss!

"I actually liked going to the orthodontist because I could have my colored rubber bands changed to fit the season! I always had orange and black for Halloween and pastel colors in the spring!"
—Naomi

"No one really noticed that I had braces until I got them off! Then everyone was like, 'What's different about you? What did you do?'"
—Sherita

Idea!

Not psyched about sporting spectacles? Try frameless glasses! They don't stand out and are very chic!

"I got glasses last month and my cousin, who is a couple of years younger, bought a pair of cheap sunglasses and poked out the plastic lenses because she wanted to look like me!"
—Regina

132

Glasses and Contact Lenses

At your annual eye appointment, you might find out you need to wear glasses. (Or you might discover the problem yourself if you are having trouble seeing the board or reading your text books.) No problem! Glasses today are so stylish that many girls and women regard them as accessories, like bracelets or earrings! Glasses can be used to highlight your favorite features. There are loads of fun choices. Often, as you are growing, your eyes change frequently, giving you lots of opportunities to pick out new frames!

Seven Secrets for Picking Out Flattering Frames

Make a statement about your looks by choosing glasses that flatter your face! Use these tips to help you.

1 Make it fun! Bring a friend or two and visit more than one eye shop. You're picking out an accessory that you'll wear everyday, so take your time and try on lots of different frames.

2 Even though you have friends to give you advice, make sure to ask a complete stranger for an opinion, too: He or she will be totally honest.

3 Think about three things when selecting your frames: style, color, and shape.

4 Select a style that shows off your personality, but that isn't too bold for every day … *and* will still appeal to you a year or two from now.

5 Don't pick out a frame that overwhelms your face. You don't want people to notice your glasses first, and then you.

6 You can use the color of your eyes to guide you toward a frame color: Brown eyes look great with turquoise, brown, black, or even bright green, jade, or lavender; blue eyes are set off nicely with light brown, turquoise, or blue tones (but not darker than your eyes); and hazel eyes look great with gold, black, or rose.

7 Pick a shape that will balance your face. (In other words, if you have a round face, don't pick round frames, pick rectangular ones.) If you're not sure what face shape you have, face the bathroom mirror and have someone trace the outline of your face on the mirror with soap. Then stand back and take a look! If you have an oval face, you're lucky! You can wear almost any shape.

You might consider contact lenses rather than glasses, especially if you are involved in sports or in activities where glasses are a bit of a nuisance. Contact lenses can be pricey, though, and they are easy to lose. If they aren't well cared for, they can hurt your eyes. It is also awkward (and painful!) if you get something in your eye or need to take them out at an inconvenient time. If your parents feel contacts are affordable for your family and you are responsible enough to care for them properly, you can ask your eye doctor about this option. Otherwise, you can wear glasses now and think about getting contacts in the future.

> "My mom would not let me get contacts because she said I wasn't responsible enough. I asked her to make a list of things that I could do that would show her that I am responsible. She wrote out a list and told me that if I consistently did everything, I could get contacts in six months. I am one month away!"
> —Janelle

Hair Care

Once you're in middle school, you may find that your hair feels a bit oilier and needs to be washed more often. Find a shampoo and a conditioner that are right for your hair type and wash your hair several times a week. Avoid brushing wet hair: That can cause damage. Instead, use a wide-tooth comb to get all the tangles out.

You want your hair to look its best all the time, but you shouldn't use a blow dryer or straightener every day. That can make your hair too dry and brittle. Let your hair dry on its own whenever possible (and look into hair products that protect hair from frequent blow drying).

In some schools, the dress code also applies to hair color and style, so before you take the plunge and dye your hair purple, make sure that won't land you a detention!

"I always have an elastic around my wrist in case my hair decides to freak out halfway through second period and I need a ponytail STAT."
—Jana

Six Steps to a Great Hair Cut

You may want to get a new haircut before starting middle school because you feel you want to move past your cute, young elementary school do. You can ask your stylist to add layers for volume and shape, or to give you a medium-length cut, which can be trendy and easy to manage. Here are some other tips for getting a great cut:

1 Cut out photos from magazines so that you can show the stylist exactly what you want. (Cover the model's face to make sure that it's the *hair* you like!) It's hard to describe a haircut but easy to point to a picture. Be realistic—don't ask for a cut that works with thick, curly hair if yours is fine and straight.

2 Don't choose a cut that requires a lot of styling before school or a lot of frequent haircuts that will end up being expensive. Think about how much time and money you can realistically devote to your hair.

3 Choose a stylist you trust, and then listen to her advice. She knows what type of hair you have, what the texture is like, and how thick it is. She will be able to guide you toward a super cute cut!

4 Talk to the hair stylist as she cuts your hair. Don't be afraid to stop her and ask a question or make a comment. As long as you are polite, you should say what's on your mind to make sure you get the cut you want!

5 Be aware that a cut should take at least a half an hour. Any less and your stylist has not done a thorough job.

6 If you don't like what you look like leaving the salon, try washing your hair at home and styling it yourself. Experiment with headbands, scarves, and barrettes. If it doesn't look any better, have your mom or dad drive you back to the hair salon and ask to have it cut again. Most hairdressers want you to be happy so that you'll recommend them to your friends.

Idea!

Do you want to give yourself a virtual makeover? Visit http://www.seventeen.com/hair-skin-makeup/salon-virtual makeover, upload your photo, and try on all sorts of different hairstyles and makeup looks!

Pierced Ears

Many middle school girls have pierced ears. (In fact, ear piercing goes back thousands of years!) If you decide to follow this fashion trend, have an adult take you to a professional. Don't ever let your friend pierce your ears! She won't have sterile equipment and hasn't had appropriate training. Nothing is as uncomfortable and ugly as red, oozing piercings, with one hole higher than the other! Someone who works at a salon or jewelry store (or even your pediatrician) will probably wear sterile gloves and will use sterile equipment to do the job, which means that an infection is less likely.

It might be a good idea for you to watch another customer go first so that you know that the right procedures are followed and you know what to expect. Rather than a needle, a piercing gun is often used. The gun uses a sterile earring to make the hole in your ear, which guarantees that germs won't be transmitted from someone else's ears to yours.

The first earrings that you will wear will probably have gold posts, which are less likely to cause an infection. These will stay in for up to six weeks to make sure that the holes won't close up when you take them out.

You will be sent home with instructions to care for your piercings. You'll probably be told to clean your ears several times a day. First, you'll wash your hands very, very well (and you'll never touch your ears unless you've just washed your hands). Then you will use a cotton ball or a cotton swab to wipe the sterile solution recommended by the piercing professional onto the area that was pierced. You'll gently turn the earrings so that they don't get stuck to your skin as the piercings heal.

Top Tip

Don't use hydrogen peroxide or rubbing alcohol to clean your piercings! There are better, pain-free solutions out there, like H2Ocean. Ask your piercer what she recommends.

Tell your mom or dad if your ears get infected. You'll know they're infected if your ear lobes are swollen, red, and sore. You may notice puss in the area of the piercing. Infections are not uncommon, but they must be dealt with right away.

The Pierced Look Without the Pain

Interested in trying out the look of pierced ears before jumping in and actually doing it? Magnetic earrings keep a metal stud in place with a magnet behind the ear lobe holding it securely. Stick-on earrings have adhesive on the back so that they stick directly to the ear. Spring hoop earrings stay on the ear because of the pressure of the spring mechanism.

"I bought three pairs of really cute but really *cheap* earrings that made my piercings infected! It was gross! I found out that I have to spend a little more money and get the kind that are especially for sensitive ears and won't cause a reaction."
—Kyra

For Healthy Nails...

• Use an emery board to shape your fingernails, and file in only one direction.

•Don't share your emery board or nail clippers with your friends.

•Use moisturizing lotion on your hands and nails.

•Eat a healthy diet to keep your nails firm, flexible, and glossy.

•Use fingernail polish remover sparingly because it dries out your nails.

•Trim your toenails after you take a shower, when the nails are easiest to cut.

Idea!

Ear cuffs are trendy and don't require pierced ears! An ear cuff is a curved piece of jewelry that is pinched into place on the side of the ear. It can be pulled apart just enough to remove it easily.

For Fun and Funky Nails...

• Use a clear base coat before applying the color and add a final coat of clear polish to seal and protect the color.

• Use a bright color as a base, then add a design in a lighter color just to your thumbs.

• Go with a zebra theme by painting black stripes on top of neon colors.

• Apply nail gel to any part of the nail where you'd like glitter to stick (like the tips), then dust the nail with glitter, shake off the excess, and allow to dry. Finally, apply a clear topcoat.

• Apply a fun base color, then add lighter colored polka dots.

• Try acrylic craft paint rather than expensive polish to add designs!

• Use a toothpick or hairpin to add swirls and dots and a nail art pen to draw a design.

• Make a center dot, then a circle of dots in another color around it to create a flower.

• Apply jewels and stickers to your nails with nail glue (then apply a clear topcoat of polish).

Makeup Secrets

Once you get to middle school, you may want to experiment with makeup. In an online survey (in which the average age of the survey takers was 13), 92 percent said they wore makeup sometimes; about 20 percent of those wore makeup to school. Most girls said they wore makeup because it made them feel prettier and more confident. (When asked how long they spent putting on their makeup, the majority of girls said less than one minute!)

You don't need to wear a lot of makeup for a beauty boost! Foundation is not necessary for pre-teens; you can put a dot of concealer on the occasional pimple and then dust some loose powder on your face if you'd like. (You might want to keep an extra concealer in your locker for those occasional touch-ups throughout the day.)

Fun FAcT

Some girls feel very strongly that they do not want to use products that were tested on animals. For more information on this subject, check out **http://www.mercyforanimals. org/cosmetic_testing.asp.**

You can also brush on a bit of pink or peach blush. Smile broadly, then apply the blush to the highpoints of your cheeks, brushing from your nose out toward your ear. You can even lightly brush some color onto your nose and chin.

Lip gloss in clear or in a neutral color is best for daytime. You can start out with products that are clearly meant for pre-teens, like Lip Smackers. Keep some with you during the day so that you can add a little shimmer to your lips after lunch.

Eye shadow may be excessive for school, especially when you are just entering middle school. If you want to wear eye shadow, try earth tones (like brown and gray) which are subtle enough for school and look good with eyes of all colors.

Brownish/black mascara works better for girls with fair hair and skin than black mascara, which can look too harsh for school. You'll probably want waterproof mascara so that it won't rub off if you get sweaty during gym class! (You will need a special remover for waterproof makeup.)

Use an eyeliner that works like a pencil and makes a smudgy line (rather than one that is more like a marker and makes a very distinct line). Use a Q-tip to blend in the line to that it isn't too defined.

When you're all done putting on your makeup, stand near a window in natural light and hold up a mirror. This is the only real way to make sure you've put on the right colors and right amount of makeup.

Makeup Swaps

Mom and Dad won't let you wear makeup yet? No sweat! There are all sorts of things you can do to feel good about your appearance. Focus on putting together cute outfits and coming up with trendy hairstyles. Eat well and exercise regularly, which will make your skin glow. Use a dab of Vaseline or a flavored lip balm (for chapped lips) to make your lips moist and shiny. And ask your mom or older sister to help you pluck stray hairs between and around your eyebrow line.

HOT OR NOT?

What's hot: Shiny lip gloss
What's not: Bold lipstick

What's hot: Body glitter that shimmers
What's not: Body glitter that sparkles

What's hot: Nails with funky designs painted on them
What's not: Nails that are so long that you can't do anything for fear of breaking them

"I really like this girl Rowan in my homeroom because she wears really cool, expensive clothes but she doesn't make kids who aren't dressed like her feel bad. She compliments me all the time on my hand-me downs from my sister!"
—Sylvia

Fun FAcT

In response to a survey conducted by the Girl Scouts, 80 percent of pre-teens said they were not at all worried about having cool clothes.

Fashion Secrets

Fashion can be fun, as long as you don't take it too seriously. It's natural to want to be admired for your clothes and your style, but you need to have enough confidence to wear what feels comfortable on you, what's right for your shape and size, and what you can afford.

You don't need to buy an entirely new wardrobe every season to keep up with the latest styles and make a fashion statement. There are a lot of ways to work a trendy piece into the wardrobe you already have. Think about spending the bulk of your budget on things you will wear a lot, like a pair of shoes or jeans that will go with lots of other pieces.

Don't head for the mall until you've check out your school's dress code! Common no-nos are spaghetti straps and short skirts, but many schools also have rules banning other items, like flip-flops and T-shirts that advertise particular products. Many girls suggest waiting to shop until after school starts. Not only will you find some great sales if you wait, but you'll have had a chance to see what looks good on other girls in your school. You don't want to look like everyone else, but you also probably don't want to look so different from everyone else that you are self-conscious.

What Are Middle School Girls Wearing Now?

Fashion trends come and go each season, but here are some staples that, according to middle school girls, are in right now:

"Moccasins, especially with old jeans."

"Outfits from Forever 21, Wet Seal, J.C. Penney, or Old Navy."

"Leopard print flats."

"A Hot Topic graphic T-shirt with flare jeans and ballet flats!"

"Two or three T-shirts and tank tops layered on top of one another."

"Patterned leggings with a cute dress."

"Cuff bracelets."

"Shirts with '70s designs, like peace signs and old cartoon characters."

"Skinny jeans!"

"Big, fun rings."

"Converse sneakers."

"Anything from Abercrombie & Fitch, or The Gap."

"A long loose top with leggings from Target."

"Clothes from American Eagle, Hollister, and Abercrombie."

"Bleached jeans that look like white paint spilled on them."

"Neon jeans."

"A stack of chunky bracelets."

"Flowered headbands like they wear on Gossip Girl."

"A Limited Too tank under an American Eagle tee."

"Flip flops, as long as your toe nails have polish."

"Brightly colored high top sneakers."

"Prints and patterns together as long as you stay with the same colors, like blues and greens."

"Pieces from H&M that are mixed and matched."

Fun FAcT

A lot of teens and pre-teens like to check out the fashions at the mall, then take those ideas to upscale second hand stores. You might find clothes just like the ones in the mall that have been gently worn (or sometimes not worn at all!) and are now half the cost!

What Does Your Zodiac Sign Say About You?

Find your birthday and read about the characteristics that go with your zodiac sign. How well do you match up with your sign?

Aries, The Ram
(March 21 – April 19)
You are creative, spontaneous, and very strong-willed. You have a warrior instinct! You are so ambitious that you can accomplish anything you set your mind to. Even though you have a temper sometimes, it's just your passionate personality coming through! You get along well with everyone, and are a loyal friend and family member.

Taurus, The Bull
(April 20 – May 20)
You are strong, stubborn, and will stand your ground until the end! Practical and patient, you are also a kind and sympathetic person. Your friends share their innermost secrets with you because you are so understanding and have a lot of common sense. You would make a great teacher or business leader.

Gemini, The Twins
(May 21 – June 20)
You are flexible, open-minded, and adaptable, and can quickly figure out what's happening in any situation and respond to it. You are sometimes hard to predict because your moods change quickly, but you are affectionate, imaginative, and generous, and your charisma is contagious. You can be just a little scatter-brained!

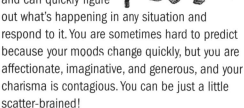

Cancer, The Crab
(June 21 – July 22)
You are all about home and family, and you love history and tradition. You want to nurture and be nurtured. Even though you can be moody sometimes, you are often quiet, and tend to hide your feelings. You are a loyal friend, but you need time alone, too. Your feelings are easily hurt.

Leo, The Lion
(July 23 – August 22)
You are a born leader, and are naturally confident and powerful. You like to voice your opinions (and you are usually right!). You are brave and stubborn, but also sensitive and loving. You might be considered bossy, but it's because you want the best for everyone around you. You like to be recognized and admired.

Virgo, The Virgin
(August 23 – September 22)
You are smart and curious, and always try to get information from others. You have a great memory and enjoy a good discussion. You like to tell people what you think about everything! You can sometimes be too hard on yourself. You make an excellent partner in any group project, and work very well with others.

Libra, The Scales

(September 23 – October 22)
You are all about balance, fairness, and stability. You like to have harmony in your life, and are a caring and understanding person. You stand up for people who can't stand up for themselves. You often don't get enough credit for the things you do because you can be quiet and shy. Even though you are introverted, you are excellent in a debate!

Scorpio, The Scorpion

(October 23 – November 21)
You are bold and confident. You are very driven, and can focus completely on a project when you want to. Even though you are forceful and determined, you are also secretive. You might like to argue about things, but that's because you think that it is healthy for everyone to see both sides of an issue.

Sagittarius, The Centaur

(November 22 – December 21)
You are intense and focused. You like to think deeply about things. You have to make sure that you don't go off in too many directions at once, though. You can be a bit impatient because you like things to happen quickly. When you fail at something, you often make an amazing comeback. You are a loyal friend, but you don't like commitment. You like a lot of space and freedom.

Capricorn, The Goat

(December 22 – January 19)
You like to think deeply about things, and are patient and very smart. You like things to be orderly and stable, and you are very organized yourself. You want to follow a plan step by step. This makes you quite productive. You tend to keep your own problems to yourself, but you take on other people's problems. You can be a little too rigid sometimes, and don't like to be criticized.

Aquarius, The Water Bearer

(January 20 – February 18)
You go about your business in a quiet, often unusual way. You think outside the box! You are smart, honest, and loyal, and you care about others very much. You make friends easily and are so relaxed you tend to be a little lazy. You are artistic and poetic, but you can be a little rebellious.

Pisces, The Fish

(February 19 – March 20)
You keep a very low profile, but you like to take in a lot of information. You are generous, trustworthy, and quiet. You tend to be very cautious and sometimes people can fool you and take advantage of you. If you believe in a cause, you are very devoted to it, and always stick up for your friends and family. You need time alone to recharge.

Chapter 7

Secrets About Life After the Bell Rings

The most interesting part of your life as a middle school student will likely be the after-school part! You may play a sport (or two!), be involved in extracurricular activities or clubs, or have a part-time baby-sitting or pet-walking job! (And of course you *have* to make time for sleepovers, outings, and hanging with friends!) All of these things are not only fun, but are worthwhile because a variety of opportunities and experiences will help you to become a more well-rounded person.

After-school Activities

Signing up for an extracurricular activity or two is a great way to make new friends and really feel like you're a part of your new school community. Think of something that interests you (art, chess, theater) and find out what your options are for after-school activities. Don't be intimidated or overwhelmed if sign-ups are the first week of school. Even though you have a lot to adjust to initially, you should still try to attend the first club meetings of the year and get all the information you can.

"I love chess, but my school didn't have a chess club. I talked to my math teacher and asked her how I could start one. She set up a meeting with the assistant principal and agreed to be the advisor. Now we meet once a week after school in her room. We have 14 kids in the club!"
—Kristen

Be careful, though, that you don't sign up for so many extra things that you start to feel stressed out! Clubs and activities are supposed to be fun, not anxiety-producing! It's great to have a busy schedule, but down time is important, too. Find out as much as you can about what is expected of club or team members before you join. Is there a weekly meeting? Are there daily rehearsals? If there are evening events, will you be able to get a ride to and from?

In general, it's best to be very involved with a small number of clubs and sports than to spread yourself too thin by jumping into a lot of activities. Many middle school girls advise that you "commit or quit." That is, either become really involved and invested in a club, or leave it all together, but don't be someone who attends half the meetings and rarely volunteers to help out. That doesn't help you and it doesn't help the organization.

Tips for Tryouts

There are many clubs and groups you can join without having to audition or try out and that's great. But some activities and sports teams can only take a limited number of kids. These will involve some sort of selection process. Although it can be nerve-wracking to try out for a school team or a play, it's one of those "life skills" that's important to master. Today you're standing on stage reading lines from *Romeo and Juliet*; in 15 years, you may be giving a presentation to the board of directors of your company. Being able to show your best self under pressure takes practice and middle school is a good time to start learning how to do this. And if you make a mistake? Nothing showcases your resilience and determination more than coming back strong from an "oops" moment. If you handle it right, the coach or teacher won't remember the mistake, just your ability to turn the mistake around!

If you don't make the cut, you'll feel very disappointed. That's natural. You may question your capabilities. You may feel jealous that some of your friends made it and you didn't. Handling rejection is hard even for adults. But try to figure out what you might do differently next time so that you *will* make it. Can you improve your swimming speed so that you'll make the team? Can you take flute lessons so that you'll make Jazz Band next year? With hard work and dedication, can you make it the next time? Remember: Jennifer Hudson didn't make it to the finals on American Idol, but four years later, she won a Grammy Award for her debut album!

There are often other ways to be involved, even if your audition or tryout didn't go as you'd planned. Sure, it's tough to be on the tech crew when you wanted to have a starring role in the play, but you are still part of the performance, and you are learning what goes on behind the scenes. Maybe you didn't make the school's soccer

Fun FAcT

Michael Jordan, one of the greatest basketball players ever, was cut from the varsity basketball team as a high school sophomore!

> "The coach knew a bunch of the girls from summer soccer and so they had a definite advantage at tryouts. At first, I was put on the B Team but I knew I was better than a lot of the girls on the A Team. I asked the coach if I could move up if I showed him that I deserved to be on the A Team. He said he'd consider it. I never missed a practice, listened to the coach's suggestions, played as hard as I could, and didn't complain. Within three weeks, I was on the A Team."
> —Fanny

team, but there are club teams in your community that you can join. You can enjoy the game, improve your skills, and perhaps make the school team next year.

Another idea is to try something completely new! Take guitar lessons if you aren't elected to Student Council; try rock climbing at the local YMCA if you are cut from the cheerleading squad. Growing up involves exploring different opportunities to see what you like and where your talents lie. It's a big, exciting world, with lots of adventures in your future!

> "All of my friends got parts in the school musical but me. I was so bummed. I sulked for over a week. Then I decided to go out for cheerleading and I love it! I am so psyched to be on the cheerleading squad! I never would have tried that if I'd gotten a part in the play!"
> —Kim

If You're Auditioning for a Play:

• Talk to other kids who have tried out for plays in the past. Ask them how the auditions are set up, what you should be prepared to do, and what advice they have.

• Try to watch the auditions before yours. If the auditions are spread out over a few days, you may be able to sit in the back of the auditorium and watch other kids to get a sense of what you should and shouldn't do.

• Ask the adult conducting the auditions if she has any suggestions as to how you can best prepare. (She'll be impressed that you are taking the tryouts so seriously!)

• If you will be required to sing or read from a prepared passage, practice! Ask your mom or dad or an older sibling to give you constructive criticism in the days before the audition so that you can improve your performance.

• On the day of the audition, relax. Remind yourself that the calmer you are, the better your performance will be. Remember that there will be other chances to try out. In many cases, the roles go to the older kids first, and some day you will be one of the older kids!

• If you don't get a part, volunteer for stage or tech crew or help with costumes. You will get an inside look at how everything works, and you will have that much more experience for the next time you try out.

I Want to Quit!

You joined the cross-country team/stage crew/art club and… you aren't having that much fun. In fact, you're thinking of quitting. You really don't want to quit… but you really don't want to stay…. AHHH! What should you do?

First of all, ask yourself why you want to quit. Some reasons are better than others. If you want to quit because you are not progressing as fast as you think you should, maybe you just need to be patient, and put forth more effort. Practice will improve your performance. If you want to quit because you don't have the best role in the musical, or the big solo in jazz band, you need to remember what it means to be part of a larger group. Others are depending on you. If you made a commitment to a group, you need to keep your word and fulfill that commitment. You can't be the star of the show every time! Take advantage of every opportunity to show the adult in charge what you're capable of, and hope that one day soon, you'll have a chance to showcase your talents.

Maybe you want to quit because there are specific things happening with your team or club that you don't like: The field hockey coach screams at the players, or the director of the marching band has scheduled practices for the next four Saturdays. Ask yourself if there is anything you can do to change what you don't like. What if your parents intervene: Will that help resolve some issues? Think about what you might be able to do to fix the problem before you decide to quit. That way, even if you end up leaving, you'll feel like you did what you could to stay.

In some cases, you may have signed up for an activity to test the waters, like horseback riding lessons or playing guitar. But you realize you aren't enjoying it. It's important to try lots of different things: You won't love everything you try. Ask yourself whether there is a natural breaking point. For instance, after the first school play has wrapped up, can you excuse yourself from stage crew? Or when marching band starts, can you take a break from your guitar lessons?

The end of a semester or a school year is often a good time to make a change. If you didn't make a long-term commitment, talk to your parents about how much notice is fair to give to a teacher or club leader.

Sometimes you simply made a mistake and over-scheduled yourself. You are so stressed out that nothing is getting done well, you are always rushing from one thing to the next, you have no free time, and you just aren't enjoying the things you're doing. It's okay to drop a commitment to give yourself more time to devote to school and the few activities that are most important to you. Every adult has had at least one experience with over-committing and then needing to cut back and simplify. Talk to your parents and explain how you are feeling. Maybe they can help you figure out how to fit everything in, or maybe they will help you talk to a coach or advisor about dropping something.

You may worry about quitting if your parents put a great deal of money into an activity or sport, such as buying you equipment or paying ahead for lessons. In that case, you need to have a heart-to-heart with them. Maybe you have a younger sibling who can take the gymnastics lessons in your place or maybe you can get credit at the tennis club that the family can put toward court time. Or you may decide that it's worth it to stick it out so that your parents will support you the next time you show an interest in something new.

Finally, you need to think about the likely consequences of quitting. Even if you're not having a super time, you may decide to finish the season because you don't want to let teammates down. If you think you may want to participate in the same activity next year, you may stick with it so that the coach or advisor doesn't have a negative impression of you.

If you do decide to quit, you need to make a graceful exit. Don't just stop showing up to practice or rehearsal. Talk to the instructor or coach in person. Make a good final impression by briefly explaining why you won't be returning. Wish a coach good luck with the season.

"You have to really think it through. I quit Robotics Club because I felt stressed out with too many after-school activities. I felt totally relieved at first because I finally had some free time. But I missed my friends from the club and then the club ended up winning regionals and going on to the state finals. I was kind of bummed for myself even though I was happy for them. I missed out on lots of fun and it would have been nice if I had some props, too!"
—Vivienne

Do You Know What Your LUCKY NUMBER Is?

Even if you already have a lucky number, you may discover you have another one you didn't even know about! (Or this may confirm that the number you've always considered lucky really is!) Grab a piece of paper, a pen, and a calculator, and take this quiz. Hopefully this number will bring you lots of luck!

- Write down the number of letters in your best friend's first name.

- Subtract the number of sisters and brothers you have.

- Add your age.

- Add the first number of your locker combination.

- Subtract the number of contacts on your cell phone or people in your address book.

- Add your homeroom number.

- Add the number of pets you have.

- Subtract your house or apartment number. If the number is negative (less than zero), make it positive. If the number is over 9, add the digits together.

What is your lucky number? _____

Birthday Parties and Other Middle School Bashes

You're too old for a princess party and too young for a cocktail party…. but you still want to celebrate your big day! What can you do with your BFFs on your birthday?

If you want to throw a party at your house, there are a lot of great tween party themes to choose from! You could plan a party based on your favorite book, TV show, movie, favorite period in history, or even your favorite color! Here are some other ideas to consider:

American Idol party: Set up a "stage" with a karaoke machine and a microphone, and decorate with blue and silver stars. Give guests contestant numbers and let them select costumes and do their makeup before performing for adult judges. Non-singers can lip sync, sing a duet, or be funny, goofy contestants.

Gypsy party: Hire someone to read palms, tell fortunes, or read Tarot cards for the party guests. Create mysterious special effects by using a smoke and fog machine and curtained tents. Make gypsy ankle bracelets as an activity, and munch on fortune cookies!

Red Carpet party: Before guests walk down the Red Carpet, adult (or older sibling) volunteers (or paid cosmetologists, if you really want to go all out!) can give party guests facials, manicures, and do their hair and makeup. Then each girl can dress as her favorite celebrity to walk down the Red Carpet as she is photographed by the "paparazzi." Interviews with the "celebs" can be videotaped and watched later, over pizza at the after-party!

Winter beach party: Beat the winter blues by putting on bikinis, playing beach ball games, and eating picnic food—indoors, of course! If guests will be sleeping over, pitch a tent in the family room, sing campfire songs, and make microwave s'mores. (You can also do the opposite: Have a winter party in the summertime by tubing down sheets of plastic under a sprinkler, having snowball fights with Styrofoam balls, and making iced "hot" chocolate!)

Paradise party: Go to a tropical paradise for your next birthday! Let your imagination take you to rain forests and exotic islands with parrots and palm trees! Create sand paintings and make tissue paper flowers with your party guests as you sip on fruit smoothies and nibble on pineapple chunks.

Craft party: Spend an afternoon with your best buds tie-dying pillowcases, making jewelry, or doing another fun craft activity. Buy everyone a white T-shirt and let each girl pick out an idea from *Generation T: 108 Ways to Transform a T-Shirt* by Megan Nicolay or buy a pack of white socks and make sock creatures following instructions from *Stupid Sock Creatures* by John Murphy.

Broadway party: Kids who love the stage can put on a play or a talent show to be performed for parents at pick-up time. Have a script ready to go, along with costumes and props, so that all your guests need to do is rehearse and prepare for the performance. For a variation on this theme, you and your friends can film it like a movie!

"A couple of my friends were really bummed that I didn't invite them to my party. I told them that my mom limited me to five guests, but I invited them to sleep over on a different night and that made it okay."
—Tina

Top Tip

To avoid hurt feelings, include the guest list with the invitation and ask your friends not to discuss the party with anyone who's not invited.

If you'd rather take your party on the road, there are lots of cool things you can do away from home! You need to plan ahead and make reservations (if you want to play laser tag, for instance), figure out transportation, plan what kinds of food and drinks to bring along, and decide how you want adults to be involved.

How about buying tickets for everyone to attend an event like a concert, play, fashion show, or sporting event? If your group would be more interested in *doing* than *watching*, head for a museum or aquarium, mini-golf course, roller rink, amusement park, a gymnastics studio where you can learn trampoline tricks, a studio where you can make pottery or stained glass, a stable where you can take a horseback ride through the woods, or even the beach!

> **"I just had an I LOVE ROBERT PATTINSON party and we played typical party games, but they all had to do with Robert Pattinson. We took photos of ourselves next to a big cardboard cut-out of him and we even ate all of his favorite foods!"**
> —Jana

Maybe you'd like to plan something even more extravagant! Consider these ideas:

Dance party: Rent a room at a community center, hire a DJ, and dance the night away! You can even set up a strobe light, hang a disco ball, or use a smoke and fog machine. Guests can dress to dance, or can dress for a certain decade, like the '50s or the '70s. If your budget will allow, hire a dance instructor to come for an hour or so and teach you the Electric Slide or other fun dance moves.

Makeover at a beauty academy: Schedule hair, manicure, and pedicure

Great Gift Ideas When You're the Guest!

It used to be easy to buy a gift when you were invited to a party in elementary school: Just grab the latest Barbie and you were good to go! But it's tougher in middle school to find a gift that is affordable and age-appropriate. Here are some great ideas:

- iTunes gift card
- Movie tickets with a box of movie candy taped to the envelope
- Makeup bag with lip balm, fingernail polish, and a cool barrette inside
- Journal and funky pens
- Photo of you and your friend together in a cool frame
- Poster of her fave celeb

appointments for your guests at a local beauty school (where the prices will be much cheaper than at a regular salon). Then have all the girls put on makeup and fancy clothes and pose for glamour shots!

Downtown scavenger hunt: If you live near a small, safe downtown, organize a scavenger hunt! Guests (on two teams) have to return home after one or two hours with items like a menu from a restaurant, a photo taken with a store owner, a receipt that someone else threw away, and a penny found face up.

> "Our house is too small for a big sleepover, but my mom always lets me have one friend stay and sleep over after my birthday party. We keep it a secret so that none of the other girls feel bad."
> —Janie

What About a Co-ed Party?

Considering having a boy/girl party now that you're in middle school? As long as your parents are ok with the idea, go for it! It's best to have a solid plan, rather than just inviting people to hang out. Middle school girls talked about their favorite co-ed parties:

"My favorite was an ice skating party at a pond with hot chocolate and donuts. It was super fun but really cold and the birthday girl opened her presents by the bonfire!"

"My friend's mom drove a big group of us to a drive-in movie. We brought sleeping bags and beach chairs and watched two shows. My friend brought snacks and drinks for everyone, too."

"We went to a place on Cape Cod where you could jump on trampolines that were built at ground level so it was totally safe. They had go-carts, too."

"The best party was at a water park. My friend's dad drove us all there and bought us tickets, then we met up for lunch and opened gifts."

"We went galactic bowling, which was bowling late at night with just black lights so that only certain things lit up. It was really fun."

"My friend Jess had a limo pick a group of us up right from school. We went to a pizza place and then the limo took us all to the movies!"

"In our city, a lot of kids have pool parties at the Best Western. You can invite lots of people, and they give you pizza and a birthday cake."

"The best time I had at a boy/girl party was at a laser tag place. It was a multi-level place and we divided our group into two teams to play. It was like a combination of tag and hide-and-seek. After, we played in the arcade. It was a blast and the boys were totally into it!"

Sleepover Secrets

Good-bye footie pjs, playing dolls before going to bed, and actually sleeping! Hello classic chick flicks, Truth or Dare, pulling harmless pranks, and staying up all night! You will be invited to lots of sleepovers in middle school, and you'll probably host a few yourself.

These are different from sleepovers in elementary school, where you might have had your best friend stay overnight in your top bunk. With your middle school friends, you'll probably have a movie marathon, pig out on yummy snack food, and take lots of goofy photos! You may blast music and dance, play Twister or Scattergories, paint your fingernails, and play flashlight tag in the neighborhood. A lot of girls hosting sleepovers plan fun crafts, too, like making friendship bracelets or decorating pillowcases.

The 10 Best Movies to Watch at a Sleepover

1　**Ten Things I Hate About You**
2　**Enchanted**
3　**Sisterhood of the Traveling Pants**
4　**Dirty Dancing**
5　**Mean Girls**
6　**She's the Man**
7　**50 First Dates**
8　**Roman Holiday**
9　**How to Lose a Guy in 10 Days**
10　**The Princess Bride**

"My little sister was so annoying when I had sleepovers! She wanted to be a part of everything! Finally my mom came up with the idea of letting her have one friend overnight when I have a sleepover. Now she doesn't bug my friends and me as much."
—Aubrey

"I remember sleeping over at my friend Leslie's house in middle school. In the morning, her dad made these weirdly shaped pancakes that he called 'road kill pancakes.'"
—Alexandra

If you're the one hosting the bash, you should know a few secrets to make things run more smoothly. You probably want to limit the time frame so that you don't get tired of being together. Believe it or not, that can happen! Ask girls to arrive around dinnertime and arrange to be picked up after breakfast the next day. Better to keep it short and sweet! Let the girls know if you'll be serving dinner (pizza is easy and popular), and plan a simple breakfast, like donuts or bagels, that your guests can manage on their own. Before your friends arrive, decide where everyone will sleep. There arc always a couple of girls who want to crash earlier than the rest of the group, so set up a place for the sleepyheads so that they can go to bed first without having an impact on the rest of the party.

Truth or Dare!

Truth or Dare is the ultimate sleepover party game! Here are a few questions and dares to get you started...

Questions:

1 What is the longest you've ever gone without taking a shower?

2 What is the one thing you want to change about yourself?

3 If you could be invisible, which person in the room would you spy on and why?

4 Of those in the room, who would you choose to spend eternity with on a deserted island?

5 If you had to choose a boy from homeroom to date, who would it be?

6 What are the deets of the most romantic dream you've ever had?

7 What are you thinking about right now?

8 What is the most embarrassing thing that ever happened to you involving a boy?

9 What was the last thing that made you cry?

10 What is the most annoying habit of the person to your right?

Dares:

1 Step outside and yodel for two minutes.

2 Drop an ice cube down your shirt and leave it there until it melts.

3 Mix three different things from the refrigerator in a glass and drink it.

4 Stuff your mouth with crackers and then go ask the nearest adult what time it is.

5 Put all of your clothing on backwards and let your friends take a photo.

6 Go outside and do cartwheels around the entire house.

7 Do the chicken dance while clucking as loud as you can.

8 Re-enact your favorite television commercial.

9 Do an imitation of the person to your left.

10 Draw a face on your stomach (with the belly button as the mouth) and make the face tell a story, moving the mouth as it "talks."

For a special occasion, you can have a sleepover somewhere besides your house, like at a hotel, campground, or even a museum!

If your parents are willing to spring for it, have them reserve two adjoining rooms in a hotel that is equipped with a pool and game room. You and your friends can take over one room (while the adults stay in the other). You can have fun in the hotel until bedtime, then watch movies and have snacks in the room. (Maybe your parents will let you order room service!)

A number of museums also have overnight packages, and you can call ahead to reserve space for your group. The museum staff generally arranges the night's activities, and takes care of food and drinks, too. In good weather, you and your friends can go camping (with parents to supervise, of course)! Maybe your family has a camper, or you can set up tents at a campsite! Read all about camping fun in Elizabeth Encarnacion's *The Girls' Guide to Campfire Activities.*

Middle Schoolers and Money

Even after you've poked among the sofa cushions, felt around the floor of the car, and rummaged around in the laundry room, you still can't come up with enough money to go to the movies or out to pizza with your friends! What's a tween to do?

Jobs

After-school or summer jobs are great because you will not only earn money, but you will learn to manage your time, you will feel more independent, and you will figure out how to deal with people of all ages in a work setting.

You may have to get a bit creative when it comes to finding a job. It can be tough to find work when you're a pre-teen, but that doesn't mean it's impossible! One option is to volunteer or intern for a business in the hopes that you will eventually be hired for a paid position. Maybe you can deliver books and magazines to patients in the hospital, help at a YMCA day care program, or shelve books at the library. If you are cheerful, hard-working, and responsible, adults will notice and you may be considered when you are a bit older and there is a job opening.

"I started volunteering in a pet store when I was 12. I did all of the crummy jobs that no one else wanted to do, like cleaning out the animal cages and scooping the dead fish out of the tanks. I did it for nothing because I love animals. When I was 14, the owner told me that if my parents would get me working papers, he'd hire me after school and on weekends, because I had proved to be such a hard worker, which he did!"

—Anya

The best option for a tween is to work for yourself! You can create flyers that describe your talents and your fees and list references (people whom a potential customer can call to ask about you). Talk to your parents about what rates you should charge, and be sure to ask their permission to deliver the flyers to friends and neighbors. There are lots of things that kids in middle school can do to earn money.

Mother's helper: A mother's helper is someone who plays and helps with children while the mom is home, but busy doing other things. This is great preparation for babysitting.

Pet walker/sitter: Are there working people in your neighborhood with dogs that need to be walked or entertained during the day? You could offer a pet sitting service after school, with washing and grooming services available for an extra fee! For regular customers, offer to take care of the family pets while they go on vacation.

House sitter: Offer to care for a neighbor's house while the family is away on vacation. You can water plants, bring in the mail and the newspaper every day, turn lights on and off so that it looks like someone is home, and let the owners know if there is an emergency at the house, like a broken water pipe.

Tutor: Are you a math whiz? Offer your tutoring services to children in elementary school. What about computers? If you know a lot about technology, you can tutor older people who may be trying to set up an email or Facebook account.

TOP TIP

If business has slowed down, print out discount coupons to remind people of your services and encourage them to call you!

Car washer: Another great way to make money is to wash cars for your neighbors: Go door to door with your own hand-held vacuum cleaner, soap, bucket, and sponge so that it will be hard for anyone to say no!

Lawnmower/gardener: You can offer to mow a neighbor's lawn, weed the garden, or trim hedges. In the spring, you can help plant a garden and offer to water it throughout the season. In the fall, ask if you can rake leaves and prepare the garden beds for the winter.

Snow shoveler: Driveways, walkways, and decks all need to be shoveled after a storm. If you can get regular clients, you will stay very busy on snow days!

Fun FAcT

Elise and Evan Macmillan, co-owners of The Chocolate Farm, are teen millionaires! They started their own business making animal-shaped chocolates, like cow lollipops, and their business is booming!

8 Great Tips Every Babysitter Should Know

Babysitting is a great way for middle school girls to make extra money! You'll be the most popular sitter in the neighborhood if you follow these tips!

1 Connect with potential families by volunteering at the church nursery or a nearby day care center. If the kids know and like you, the parents will want to hire you.

2 Take a babysitting course at the Red Cross or a similar community agency. You'll learn important ways to keep your little charges safe, and parents will be more likely to call you (especially if you get CPR certified or learn how to do the Heimlich maneuver!).

3 Create an emergency form. It should have places to write down parent contact information, phone numbers of neighbors or close relatives, and the numbers for the police and fire departments and the children's pediatrician. When you arrive at a job, ask the parents to fill out the form.

4 Have a fee in mind. When you are asked to babysit, and you agree, say, "I charge $8 an hour. Will that work for you?" You don't want to spend four hours playing Chutes and Ladders and leave with five bucks in quarters.

At some point, you will have an *OOPS!* moment on the job. Everyone does By handling things well afterward, you will not only fix the problem, but earn the respect of those you are working for. In general, you should try to offer a solution along with the problem. People will always be more receptive if you try to problem-solve before approaching them.

What if...

...something breaks when you're working in someone else's house?

Definitely don't try to hide something like this. As soon as possible, talk to the owner of the house and apologize. Offer to pay for or replace the item. If it is much too expensive, ask what you can do to make it up to them. (They may have insurance that will cover the cost.) Can you go on eBay and try to find a similar item to replace the broken one or take it somewhere to be repaired? Your parents may be able to help you determine where to find a replacement item. (In any case, don't charge for the service you were providing when you broke the item.)

...you forget to mow your neighbor's lawn when you promised you would?

As soon as you remember, head right over and offer to mow for free, or at a greatly reduced price. You want them to continue to hire you to mow, so you

5 Have a babysitting bag that you bring with you to your jobs. Fill it with special books, card and board games, toys that would appeal to a wide age range (like blocks, Play-Doh, or a cool ball), craft items to make clothespin dolls or pom pom creatures (or craft kits), and movies. Kids love new things to play with!

6 Make sure you know all of the house rules and expectations before the parents leave. Find out what the kids' normal routine is, and ask if you need to make a meal, help with homework, give medication, or any other specific task.

7 Try to enlist the help of the kids to clean up as you go along. You can make it fun by coming up with a clean-up song, or promising a special treat once things are picked up. Kids will also help wash dishes if you let them play in the soapy water. Parents love to come home to a clean house.

8 When the parents return, fill them in on anything important that happened while they were away. Never try to cover up anything that might be embarrassing, like a broken plate or a skinned knee. Parents understand that things happen. They will value your honesty.

need to reassure them that you take the job seriously and are a responsible person. By offering to take a pay cut on the job you forgot, you are letting them know that you want their repeat business.

...you get asked out on a date by your crush after you already told your neighbor you'd babysit?

See if your crush is willing to change the date. If he asked you out for Friday night, suggest Saturday. If it's a special event, like a dance, you can explain the babysitting dilemma to him. Tell him that you'll get back to him after you do a bit of problem-solving. You have a few choices. If you know the family well, you might ask if they would mind changing their date night from Friday to Saturday, or vice-versa. Another option is to ask a friend to fill in for you, and then ask the neighbors if they would mind if "Katie" babysat in your place. Offer to bring her over ahead of time to meet them as well as the kids. If none of these work, you need to honor the babysitting commitment. Remember: If he liked you enough to ask you out once, he'll ask you again for sure!

...the kids you are babysitting for behave terribly?

Your response will depend on how well you know the family. If you babysit for them frequently, and things normally go well, you can let the parents know that the kids were a bit of a challenge this time. Suggest things that you can do together that will help for the next time: "I think that if you remind the boys what their bedtime is when I arrive, it will be easier for me to reinforce it." If you are new at the job, and the kids are a real handful, you can just decide not to work for that family again. That's the beauty of babysitting! There are lots of families looking for good babysitters, so you should have your pick!

...you aren't being paid enough for the job you're doing?

You can prevent this from happening if you discuss your pay before agreeing to do the job. Be specific: You charge $8 per hour to babysit or $20 to mow the lawn. If the person you are working for tries to add other things (like weeding the garden or vacuuming the house), tell him that you'll be happy to, for an additional amount of money. You shouldn't be afraid to discuss your payment; be friendly and respectful, but firm. If you feel you're being taken advantage of by a repeat customer, write up a final bill for work you've done, and then don't work for that person again.

Top Tip

If you are offered a new babysitting job, don't agree to more than one date at first. If the kids are too difficult to manage, you don't want to have committed the next four Saturday nights to watching them!...you aren't being paid enough for the job you're doing?

An Allowance

Surveys show that between half and three-quarters of kids get regular allowances from their parents. The average weekly allowance is between 50 cents and a dollar for every year of a child's life, meaning that a 12-year old would receive between $6 and $12 a week. In most cases, the amount is dependent on what the allowance is supposed to cover.

If you'd like your parents to start giving you an allowance, explain to them that an allowance isn't a way for you to get extra spending money. It's a way for you to learn to manage the money your parents already give you for things like movies, makeup, and trips to the mall.

Sit down with your mom and dad and decide what your allowance should cover. Then you can determine how much you should receive each week. You might decide your allowance should cover entertainment and meals with friends, extra clothes (that aren't part

Should You Ask for an Advance on Your Allowance?

Asking for an advance is basically asking to borrow from your parents against money you will be getting in the future. You shouldn't borrow more than a month's worth of allowance because it will take too long to pay it back. As a general rule, you should save for something that will still be available in a few months, like an iPod, and borrow for something that you can't do a month from now, like attend a special concert or play that is happening next week. You should offer to pay your parents interest, but keep it simple. Just say you'll pay back the money plus $1.

of back-to-school shopping), birthday gifts for friends, texts on your cell phone bill, subscriptions to magazines, and iTunes purchases. Whatever the amount is, you'll have to plan your spending carefully so that you also end up with enough money to go bowling on Friday night with your buds.

Save/Spend/Give

Many financial experts suggest that kids should save half of the money they make, spend 40 percent, and give 10 percent to charity. But in reality, most kids spend twice as much as they save. To encourage savings, a number of banks have special programs where they allow pre-teens to open accounts with check-writing privileges and even ATM cards. If you think you're ready for this, talk to your parents about helping you get an account. If you don't like the idea of saving money, think of it this way: Saving is really just postponed spending. You can't earn enough money to buy a new bike in a week, but if you save it, you might be able to earn enough money in two months to buy one.

What About Credit Cards?

Middle school is a bit young to have a traditional credit card, which requires users to understand interest rates, card fees, credit limits, and credit scores. Two-thirds of *high school* students don't use credit cards. If you feel you are responsible enough to have a credit card, you'll have to prove that to your parents. Start by keeping track of your text messages and cell phone minutes, balancing your checkbook every month, and saving money in a bank account. Until your parents feel you are old enough for a traditional credit card, you can get a pre-paid card through a store like Wal-Mart. Keeping careful track of your balance on a pre-paid card is another way to show your parents how responsible you are.

What Do You Do for Extra Spending Money?

"My mom hates filling out all of the paperwork to get rebates on stuff she buys, so I fill them out in my name and the rebate check comes to me!"
—Jodi

"If I go grocery shopping with my mom and I go get all of the specific things that she has coupons for, she'll give me half of that amount back. Like, if I save her $8, she'll give me $4."
—Trenese

"I organize a garage sale in the summer, mostly for my old toys and clothes but also for stuff my parents don't want. I'm allowed to keep all of the money I make."
—Palmer

Fun FAcT

According to an online survey, 30 percent of girls (most between 12 and 13 years old) saved most of their money, 25 percent spent most of it on clothes, 12 percent said it usually went toward going out with friends, 11 percent bought food, 7 percent shelled out the most for movies or music, 5 percent put their money toward beauty products and 4 percent chose computer or video games. (The rest didn't have money to spend.)

Summertime

Summer vacation! It's unbelievably great for about a week and then... it starts to get just a *little* boring. You're too old to hang with your mom at the community pool everyday, and too young to waitress at the local hot spot. It can be hard to find ways to have fun and stay busy during summer vacation when you're in middle school.

Work

Consider pursuing one of the jobs mentioned in the section on money, above. There are often more opportunities for work during the summertime than during the school year. In the summer, you can offer to watch kids for parents who work during the day, especially if your own mom is just a few houses away. You can also be a mother's helper for summer outings, such as a day at the beach, where a mom often needs an extra pair of hands.

Volunteer

Helping others can be a great way to spend some of your vacation. Not only will you feel good about what you're doing, but you'll learn important skills that you can use someday in a paying job. In some cases, a volunteer job will lead directly to a paid position when you're older.

You'll find many volunteer opportunities in your community. Offer to help out at the library, as a junior camp counselor, walking dogs for a vet or pet store, cleaning up the local park, or making meals at the local soup kitchen.

In some cases, you won't be able to volunteer without a parent to supervise you. In that case, you'll have to think about other ways you can help. If the local animal shelter won't let you

5 Fun Books to Read Over Summer Vacation

- *The Sisterhood of the Traveling Pants* (series) by Ann Brashares
- *Angus, Thongs and Full-Frontal Snogging* by Louise Rennison
- *The Clique* (series) by Lisi Harrison
- *A Walk to Remember* by Nicholas Sparks
- *Ella Enchanted* by Gail Carson Levine

volunteer because you are too young, for instance, think about what else you can do. Can you collect old blankets or towels for the animal cages? Have a car wash or a garage sale to raise money for dog food or cleaning supplies? Ask them what they need and think of ways you can help.

Volunteering is always more fun when you do it with friends. Together, you and your friends can make fleece blankets to give to foster kids, or write letters to your congressmen and women about causes you feel strongly about. If you want to help, you will find a way!

Learn Something New

Your local recreation or community center is a great source of tween activities. Check into art, music, and dance classes. Ask about field trips to sporting events, plays, museums, and even overnight destinations. Often, a rec center will offer sports programs in the summer; you can join a tennis or basketball league. Many

Idea!

Find out all about Global Youth Service Day, a day that celebrates young people changing the world through volunteerism at http://www.gysd.org/.

cities have public pools that are operated by the recreation center and staffed with lifeguards. Ask your mom or dad to pick up a brochure that lists summer activities or check it out online.

Your local public library will also offer a range of programs for kids in the summer. In addition to summer book clubs, they may offer free movies, chess and board game tournaments, museum trips, and many other interesting things.

Be a Camper

Forget about fun-on-the-farm camp! That was *so* fourth grade! As a middle schooler, you'll be checking out camps for engineering, computers, inventing, photography, theater improv, tennis, and all sorts of other cool things!

If you aren't ready to spend a week or two away from home, if you've never been to camp, or if your family is on a tight budget, opt for day camp. Your local newspaper will probably publish a list of camps in your area as summer nears, and schools will send home flyers advertising camps in town.

You can choose from a number of different types of day camps. Traditional camps have programs that will involve everything from arts and crafts to outdoor games. Academic camps might take place at a nearby college and will focus on a particular area of interest, like marine biology camp, creative writing camp, or math camp. Camps specializing in creative arts will have programs in the theater, fine arts, or music. Your church or synagogue may have a day camp that will combine religious activities with traditional camp fun. Sports camps help you improve your skills in a particular athletic area, like soccer, golf, or cross-country running. Outdoor adventure camps are for kids who like to kayak, rock climb, go white water rafting, and caving.

Whether you choose day camp or overnight, you may be tempted to sign up with a friend. That can be great… or not so great. You will be less anxious if you have a friend with you, and you won't have to spend the first few days trying to figure out who to hang out with. But the fun of going to camp is not just doing exciting things, but meeting new people. It's hard to force yourself to make new friends if you already have a friend with you.

If you choose overnight camp, you have a wide selection. There are wilderness trips through Vermont, performing arts camps in New York, circus camps in California, and space camps in Florida! In some cases, you might be living in rustic cabins with outhouses, and in others, in college dorms! Ask yourself how far from home you want to be, how long you want to be at camp, and what kind of camp experience you're looking for. You'll also need to decide if you

want to go to an all girls' camp or a co-ed one. It might seem like fun to camp with boys, but sometimes girls have more fun together without boys around.

"I went to a music camp that wasn't very far from my house, but there were kids from all over the world there! We slept in cabins and gave concerts in this big barn."
— Alyson

"I went to a church camp in the White Mountains with about eight kids from my youth group. We did tons of things, from rock climbing to archery to making jewelry. It was really fun and I am still in touch with three or four girls from other churches."
— Josie

It's always best to visit the camp the summer before you go so that you can see for yourself what it's like. The next best thing is to talk with someone who has gone there before. Ask specific questions about what the camper liked or didn't like.

Once you've chosen your camp, you'll get a packet with forms to fill out and a list of items to bring. You might want to find out if you can bring posters or photos to hang up in your cabin or room. Bring pre-stamped post cards so that you can write a quick note to your parents if you miss them. Also find out what the rules are about care packages. If they are allowed, ask your parents to send enough snacks and goodies so that you can share.

To make your camp experience a success, you need to go with a great attitude. Even if you feel a little embarrassed, jump right into the get-to-know-you activities that the counselors organize. Embrace the camp traditions: songs, activities, and rituals. When you have a choice, choose an activity over R&R (rest and relaxation) time. You might have to go outside of your comfort zone, but you'll be glad you did.

You may be a little homesick when you first get to camp, but so will a lot of the other kids. It's very normal to miss your home and family. It's good to have a little taste of being away from home so that when you have school trips in high school and then go away to college, you will have had some experience with being independent. Try to go with a positive attitude and keep things in perspective: It's only a week or two after all. You can buck up and find ways to have fun, even if things aren't exactly as you expected. Try to distract yourself from feelings of sadness by staying busy. You might find that when you leave camp and go home, you miss the friends, counselors, and routine from camp! (You'll want to get everyone's phone number and instant messenger names before you leave!) And if you stick it out, you'll look back and be proud that you did.

Middle School Bucket List

Do you remember the movie **The Bucket List**? An old man (played by Morgan Freeman) decides to keep a list of all of the things he wants to do before he "kicks the bucket." Maybe you have some things that you want to do before you leave middle school. Here are a few suggestions, and a place to jot down your own list.

Ideas for a middle school bucket list:

 Dress for a dance with a funky theme in mind. Grab four friends and go to the next middle school dance dressed up as, say, the Spice Girls! Take lots of pics for posterity.

 Try every item in the vending machine.

Audition for the talent show with a group of friends... even if you don't think you have talent! Anyone can juggle scarves, learn a few jump rope or hula-hoop tricks, or put together some dance moves to a favorite song!

Eat at every single table at the cafeteria.

> "Whenever there were band concerts, big risers were set up on the stage. It was one of our goals that before we left middle school, my friends and I would sneak out of the cafeteria with our lunches and eat under the risers because they created kind of a cool little hideout, like a cave. We were all such 'good girls' that we kept putting it off because we were afraid of getting in trouble. We finally did it just before the final Jazz Band concert in eighth grade. It wasn't exactly what we expected because it was kind of dark and musty under there, but we were really proud of ourselves for being brave enough to do it... And we didn't get caught!"
>
> —Alex

 Host a formal party at your house. Ask your friends (guys and girls) to dress in their best! Serve them fancy hors d'oeuvres and sparkling cider in champagne glasses. Take photos! (Guests can bring pajama pants so that at the end of the party, everyone can change, chill, and watch a movie or listen to music!)

 Go to a sporting event just to cheer on a friend.

Offer to host the class pet over a vacation.

Befriend a teacher or other adult at the middle school so that in the years to come, you have someone special to visit—someone who will be really excited to hear about your future accomplishments.

My own middle school bucket list:

1 _____

2 _____

3 _____

4 _____

5 _____

6 _____

7 _____

8 _____

9 _____

10 _____

Chapter 8

Secrets from Girls Who Are Older and Wiser

"My number one piece of advice is to remember that middle school doesn't last forever, although there are totally days when it feels like it does. But those three years go by so fast, and before you can believe it, you're heading off to high school. All of a sudden, your archenemy turns into one of your best buds because you end up working together after school at Friendly's. You look back and realize that the things you saw as huge, overwhelming problems ended up having no real impact on your life at all. I wish I could take back the days I spent being upset over something that didn't even matter a week later!"

—Lisa

You could probably write a great book for kids starting out in elementary school. You know what you liked and didn't like, what you would do all over again (the jump rope club) and what you would avoid at all costs (Mrs Baird's science class). In a few years, you'll be an expert on middle school, too. Unfortunately, there's no shortcut to experience. You can't just instantly know your way around the school perfectly and know everybody's name and understand the social dynamics inside and out. It all takes time. But it's going *through* something—and not around it—that makes us stronger and more capable of handling the next challenge.

When you look back on middle school, you'll have all sorts of secrets to share with younger sisters, cousins, or friends. Here's some advice that older girls want to share with you…

"In middle school I was jealous of the girls who told stories about playing truth or dare with boys because they seemed to get a lot of attention from the guys in my class and it always sounded like they had a lot of fun. Later I realized that the guys were only into it because they could push those girls to do pretty much *anything*... they didn't respect or even like those girls at all. Looking back, I'm really glad I steered clear of those 'truth or dare' parties..."
—Cassie

"I would tell girls in middle school to appreciate the fact that their grades don't count toward college. As soon as I got into high school, I wanted to go back to middle school where my grades were really only important to my parents and me! I wished I had appreciated the middle school years more because they are kind of your last years to be a kid."
—Melissa

"My mom always knew which girls would turn out to be solid friends and which ones would end up hurting me. The girl she liked the best when I was in middle school ended up being my roommate in college!"
—Corinne

"It wasn't until I was older that I realized that coolness in middle school is based on totally random stuff! I remember that it was cool to buy these certain cookies for 50 cents at lunch and so I bought one every single day even if I didn't want it. Isn't that crazy? What a waste of money!"
—Bianca

"I remember this girl named Helena from my class in middle school. She was nice and smart, but she wore outfits that were nothing like what the other girls wore and she was super tall and skinny. She didn't care about boys or makeup and she sat alone every single day at lunch reading a book. At the time, I was just glad that wasn't me. I wasn't confident enough to reach out to her because of what it might do to my social status. We had our five-year high school class reunion recently. Helena was there and she dressed exactly like she had in middle school, but she looked fantastic to me! She had majored in theater in college and was living in New York and getting ready to be in a Broadway play. She's a total winner... and I feel like my friends and I were the losers for not realizing that."

—Mel

"I remember thinking it was cool to hate your mom and to spend as little time as possible at home. All of the popular girls at school would complain about how 'lame' or 'unfair' their moms were. I would randomly pick fights with my mom because that's what preteens are 'supposed to do.' Looking back, I realize that I was never happier than when my mom and I were getting along. She would give me thoughtful, good advice, I was grateful when I could confide in her, and she was always willing to drive me and my friends to the movies, the mall, or anywhere else we wanted to go. There is definitely nothing cool about hating your parents, not in middle school and not now! As far as I'm concerned, there's nothing cooler than being BFFs with your mom."

—Alexa

"The coolest girl when I was in middle school was named Nikki. She ruled the social scene. She could be so nasty and mean, but she had a group of girls who just worshipped the ground she walked on. I hate to admit it, but I was in awe of her. I remember my mom asking me what was so special about her and I didn't really know! She had created this mystique around her and we all bought into it. I lost track of her after eighth grade. A few days ago, my friends took me out to dinner because I'm heading off to Paris for my junior year in college. Guess who our waitress was? Nikki! I said hello and asked what she was up to and she basically said she had dropped out of high school and had been waitressing ever since because she didn't know what she wanted to do with her life. None of my friends said anything about it, but we didn't have to. I know we were all thinking the same thing."

—Dakota

"During middle school I always felt like I *needed* to have a boyfriend, like if I didn't have a boyfriend people would think I was a loser or maybe I would never get a date in high school if I didn't start dating in middle school. Looking back, I don't even remember who dated who in middle school and neither do any of my friends. My greatest memories are nights I spent hanging out with friends, not the few 'dates' that I went on with boys. Dating in middle school can be fun, but it definitely isn't the big deal that people think it is at the time. Definitely NOT worth stressing over!"

—Courtney

About
the Author

Cynthia Copeland is the
best-selling and award-winning
author of more than 25 books
for parents and children.
Her work has been featured
on Good Morning America,
selected for Oprah's "O List"
in *O Magazine*, and featured
in parenting magazines. Cindy
has sold over three-quarters of
a million books in at least five
languages; her *Really Important
Stuff My Kids Have Taught Me*
has sold 400,000 copies alone.
She currently lives in New
Hampshire with her family.

About Applesauce Press

What kid doesn't love Applesauce?

Applesauce Press was created to press out the best children's books found anywhere. Like our parent company, Cider Mill Press Book Publishers, we strive to bring fine reading, information, and entertainment to kids of all ages. Between the covers of our creatively crafted books, you'll find beautiful designs, creative formats, and most of all, kid-friendly information on a variety of topics. Our Cider Mill bears fruit twice a year, publishing a new crop of titles each spring and fall.

"Where Good Books Are Ready for Press"

Visit us on the Web at
www.cidermillpress.com
or write to us at
12 Port Farm Road
Kennebunkport, Maine 04046